AMERICA'S SOCCER HERITAGE
A HISTORY OF THE GAME

by
SAM FOULDS
PAUL HARRIS

Cover design
by
RON NORRIS

SOCCER FOR AMERICANS
Box 836
Manhattan Beach, California 90266

DEDICATION: TO OUR WIVES

ELIZABETH W. FOULDS, who has supported me wholeheartedly in my soccer activities and research for fifty years.

DORIS V. HARRIS, who continues to encourage me, though from time to time she may wonder if I've headed too many soccer balls.

This book is a
gift to the Library
from

Paul Harris

ISBN 0-916802-14-0
Library of Congress Catalog Number 79-63981

Copyright © 1979 Soccer for Americans
Box 836 Manhattan Beach, California 90266

Introduction

The result of a soccer game is not the end of the world, and the history of American soccer is not exactly the history of America. However, the United States is a nation of immigrants, and soccer was a pastime of many of these people. It was a game that provided diversion, and sometimes unpleasantness, for large numbers of people who had come in search of something different. As is true today, most played without giving much thought to the future or to the past of the game. Soccer provided momentary joy and accomplishment, and playing the game was most important.

History books can be consumed by those who prefer to live in the past or by those who wish to understand the present. A glance behind at American soccer is enlightening, particularly if we want to avoid repeating some mistakes. While the game suffered and struggled, largely because of ill-planning and giant egos, it was still held dear by a sprinkling of individuals with unusual foresight.

This book was written to settle, once and for all, the argument over America's soccer heritage. Although most players received little real coaching, it was an American coach, George Matthew Collins, who developed the first real innovation in defensive soccer. Americans, always energetic and never satisfied, introduced rule changes which were finally adopted by the world. American referees and players were sought for duty in Europe and South America. Our soccer heritage is varied, rich, and deserving of notice by all who really care about the game.

Television, modern communication, printed matter, and countless clinicians have taught us much about the game, and the average youngster has seen the greatest players, and is seeking to imitate all the techniques. As America quickly moves down the road toward quantity and quality, it should look, though briefly, at those people and events who brought us this far.

Finally, our sincerest apologies and regrets to the many coaches, players, referees, and organizers who are not included. We, and the game, are indebted to you all.

The true spirit of soccer is shown in many ways. It just depends on whom you're talking to, or watching.

Table of Contents

Chapters

1

SOME ORIGINS
Before the United States

An early game in England, with large crowds in attendance. Note the markings on the field and the similarity of the uniforms.

1

Football is a word that has many connotations, depending upon the area of the world in which you are located and to whom you are speaking.

To the average American sports fan football is the name of the game that evolved in the colleges of the United States from English rugby roots and developed into a distinctive pastime indigenous with America. There are many facets to football in general. The Australians have their Australian Rules game, which is a combination of rugby, Gaelic football and soccer. The Irish have their Gaelic football with soccer overtones and the British have both soccer and rugby. Yet in all the world the Association game, known popularly as soccer, is the accepted and predominately kicking sport, the one most appropriate for the appellation of football.

All of the variations of football have similar antecedents in common and all have their true origin in Medieval times, when the sport was a form of mob exercise. It was a pastime bred in violence, dangerous to life and property. It was practiced by the commoners in England as a form of amusement and served as a relief valve to liven up their dreary lives.

Football in its infancy wore a coat of many colors. It was a sport without a set of coordinated rules and in its ambiguity it could be considered the father of all the species of the game that have survived until the present day. During the nineteenth century football was propagated in its many forms in the Public (private) schools and universities of England and in the colleges and preparatory schools of the United States. It was a development that produced many missionaries among the sports oriented members of the middle and upper classes of society.

In Victorian England, football, a direct descendent of the robust village and town game, made its advent in the British private schools as a regular part of the curriculum. The trend soon caught the enthusiasm of the ordinary workmen and tradespeople, who with the benefits of the burgeoning industrial revolution were emerging into an era of more leisure time.

In the Greater London area Association football or soccer served as an outdoor pastime for the socially elite Public school and university students and graduates, all of whom were affluent. Meanwhile in the industrial districts such as Sheffield and the Lancashire towns as well as other hinterland communities it was to emerge as a game for the commoner.

The gathering of football clubs from the environment of London at the Freemason's Tavern in London on October 23, 1863, when the Football Association was formed, has received general acclaim as the birthplace of modern soccer, but other areas were equally active in bringing order out of chaos. Sheffield footballers in the Midlands of England during the same period were making rapid progress among a more mundane clientele from the working classes. It was a joining together of all these impulses and traditions that eventually produced the modern soccer code.

2
A GAME CALLED PASUCKQUAKKOHOWOG

The beach at Lynn, Massachusetts, where the Indians became America's first soccer players.

2

British soccer can trace its early beginnings to the mob football as played by the peasants of medieval England and Scotland. American soccer also has an ancient background of its own.

In America, where soccer until recently has been somewhat of a step-child in its relationship to the rest of the sporting world, the native Indians were already engaged in a booting game that closely resembled soccer as it was played in the "Old Country." When the Pilgrims arrived at Plymouth Rock in 1620, they found the Indians playing a game called "Pasuckquak-kohowog," which in English could be translated into, "They gather to play football."

According to Charles C. Willoughby, in his *Commonwealth History of Massachusetts* the game of football was one of the favorite pastimes of the Indians. William Wood was an early settler in Lynn on the North Shore of Massachusetts and in Sandwich on Cape Cod. In his *New England Prospect* published in 1634, he also left an account of this sport:

> "Apparently, the tribes of New England were the only Indians on the continent of North America who played this type of ball game. Usually, the Indians played football during the summer months with a varying number of players involved, depending upon the cir-cumstances. Village played against village and a large amount of property changed hands, depending upon the outcome of the game. Surprisingly, there was little quarreling."

More often than not the venue for a game was on a broad sandy beach at Lynn, Revere or Cape Cod, where playing surfaces approximately a mile long and a half mile wide on hard sand were available at low tide. Goal posts were placed at each end of the playing area. The goals were sometimes a mile apart and the football was about the size of a handball. It had a cover of deerskin, stuffed with deer hair. If a game carried over one day to the next, the ground would be remarked.

Although thirty to forty men on a side was often the full complement of player strength, at times as many as 1,000 people might participate in the activity. Instead of donning a uniform the Indians covered themselves with paint and ornaments as if planning to do battle. In this way no one, opponent or teammate, could be identified. It was not uncommon for legs or other bones to be broken during the course of a game and the disguise made it possible for the one who was responsible for the accident to escape detection. In this way retaliation was unlikely.

Before the start of the game the players disarmed themselves by hanging their weapons on the nearby tree branches. A long line was drawn upon the sand midway between the two goals, over which the contending parties shook hands.

The Indians were very agile and fast on their feet. William Wood, who was an occasional on-looker, was entranced by the tactics of the players but his preference was for games in which few players took part in order that he could appreciate better their "swift footmanship, their strange manipulation of the ball and their plunging into the water to wrestle for the ball."

However, he was not impressed by their technique or their strategy and boasted that "One Englishman could beat ten Indians at football." Whenever the teams were of equal strength it would take two or three days to determine a winner.

For an important contest, the goal posts would be laden with trophies such as wampum, beaver, otter and other skins. A prize so valuable caused Wood to write, "It would exceed the belief of many to relate the worth of one goal." The Indians by nature were fond of gambling. Betting was done before the game and was usually overseen by the more influential and older men of the tribe. Often an Indian would wager everything that he owned on the outcome of a single game. Clothes, food, knives, wampum and even his tribal standing were his collateral.

The atmosphere at important games assumed a most festive mood, with feasting, dancing, betting and a general good time added to the enjoyment of young and old. Roger Williams, the founder of Rhode Island, abhored the gaiety of these affairs as "I feared the distractions of the games, and would not attend them in order that I might not countenance and partake of their folly after I saw the evil of them." During the game the families, relatives and friends formed cheering squads along the sidelines. The women and girls would dance and sing, while the boys provided the accompaniment blowing on hollow reeds and the beating of sticks together. Following the game everyone sat down to a bountiful repast and vibrant merrymaking before returning home.

3
BASEBALL AND SOCCER
Strange Bedfellows

Baseball and soccer got together in 1894. The experiment was short-lived, and a setback for soccer. This Washington team fared better than their soccer club.

3

Professional soccer has enjoyed a long and varied career. Of the popular team games in the United States only baseball can boast an earlier appearance.

The abundance of immigration from Britain and Ireland during the 1880's "accelerated the growth of soccer in America and brought about the formation of the American Football Association at Newark, N.Y. in 1884. Before that date, except for an abortive attempt by the eastern colleges in the 1870's to popularize the game, soccer was a spasmodic and poorly organized activity played almost exclusively by the working people in manufacturing and industrial areas.

It was not until 1888 that professionalism came of age in England with the organization of the English League, long after professional baseball in the United States had reached the same stage. The decision of the Football Association of England to recognize the professional element in 1885 had laid the groundwork for a professional league venture. It was an historic moment for the sport after years of controversy, and it elevated professional soccer to a stable and respected position in the athletic world.

Amateur soccer towards the end of the nineteenth century had become a recreational outlet for most immigrants from Britain and Ireland in America. Neo-professionalism did exist among some clubs that were able to provide jobs or liberal expense money as an inducement. The first hint of real professional activity among American soccer men did not occur until 1891, when a Canadian All-Star team made its second of two visits to the British Isles.

Several American players were with the Canadian squad on this overseas tour, which was financially speculative. The team played a busy schedule of fifty games from August 1891 until January 1892. The competition was furnished by professional league teams and international elevens from England, Scotland, Ireland and Wales. At the conclusion of this unusual jaunt several of the players were persuaded to remain in

England and join English League clubs, while the remainder of the squad returned to America.

It was in 1894, only six years after professional league soccer emerged in Britain, that the American League of Professional Football (Soccer) Clubs came into existence along the Eastern seaboard. It was an ambitious plan and poorly conceived in scope, but it did introduce professional soccer to the United States with a major league background.

To the founders of the league, the baseball entrepreneurs of the Eastern Division of the National Baseball League, the idea of a complementary soccer operation appeared to be a sound and desirable business promotion that would keep their stadiums continually occupied and productive after the end of the baseball season in October. Baltimore, Boston, Brooklyn, New York, Philadelphia and Washington, the Eastern clubs of the National Baseball League, were issued franchises in the new soccer league. It was reasoned that the Eastern cities with their large soccer-oriented populace would immediately become ardent supporters of professional soccer and would create a nucleus upon which to build enthusiasm for the game among native-born sports followers.

Managers of the professional baseball teams were drafted to assume the dual role of coaches for the soccer clubs, even though they had little or no knowledge of the game. Only Baltimore was directed by a soccer coach. Frank Selee of Boston, John Ward of New York, Artie Irwin of Philadelphia, Gus Schmelz of Washington and Dave Foutz of Brooklyn all tried hard to produce winning teams but they had neither the know-how nor the caliber of material available to combat the more sophisticated talent of the Baltimore Orioles. The Baltimore team, managed adroitly by Ned Hanlon, sought an advantage on the other league members by going across the Atlantic to import a professional coach from England, A. W. Stewart. Through his overseas connections Stewart was able to bring to the United States eight prominent English professional players from the Manchester district of Lancashire.

Meanwhile, the other teams in the new American League had not been idle. Most of them had acquired recruits from the ranks of the many professional players who had immigrated on permanent visas to the United States to align themselves with industrially sponsored soccer clubs. Many professional players from Scotland, England and Ireland found that playing soccer in the United States could be more lucrative to them, for no salary limitations were in vogue.

Teams relied on local amateur and professional players of proven ability to round out their playing strength. A notable example of the gathering together of talent from local sources was exemplified by the Boston team. This club drew heavily upon such nearby soccer hotbeds as Fall River, Pawtucket, Quincy, Providence and Lawrence, all textile communities, with large immigrant soccer-educated populations. At the time these cities and their areas boasted of many of the finest teams in the nation.

The American League of Professional Football Clubs officially opened its season on October 6, 1894 with the Boston Beaneaters, the New York Giants, the Washington Senators, the Baltimore Orioles, the Philadelphia Quakers and the Brooklyn Superbas comprising a well knit group. The regular admission charge at the games was a modest twenty-five cents, financially within reach of the ordinary working man. All of the teams were operated by the National Baseball League clubs in their respective cities.

On opening day, Boston defeated Brooklyn, 3-2 at the South End Grounds in Boston while in New York City at the Polo Grounds the Giants won over Philadelphia by a 5-0 score. The new soccer venture of the baseball professional interests was received enthusiastically by the *Washington Post.*

"Reports from Philadelphia and Boston indicate that the new game will be a big success. The playing of the four teams was of a character to stir up lots of enthusiasm and excitement."

Twelve days later, on October 18th, Boston defeated New York 4-3 at the Polo Grounds in New York before a slim gathering of fewer than 100 fans. The attendance was not surprising as the game was played on a Thursday afternoon when the bulk of the potential soccer crowd was working.

The failure of the promoters to realize that the basic support in the initial stages of the league rested with the large soccer addicted foreign-born blue collar working population of the Eastern industrial states was unfortunate. A little application of common sense would have told them that the ordinary wage earner was available only Saturday afternoons and Sundays. Also, the failure to coordinate the opening of the soccer season with the conclusion of the Temple Cup series, the National Baseball League playoffs, imposed a self inflicted conflict of interest that was difficult to offset.

The Temple Cup games, which involved New York and Washington, held up the debut of the Baltimore and Washington clubs. When the Senators did get underway, they won their first contest from Philadelphia by 2 goals to 1 but unfortunately they failed to win another league game. In the Baltimore versus Washington encounter which introduced professional soccer to Baltimore the home team won easily by a 5 to 1 tally. The *Baltimore Sun* gave considerable space to the game and commented:

"A crowd estimated to contain 8,000 persons saw yesterday the first professional football game ever played in Baltimore. The team defeated Washington 5-1 and the spectators rooted with delight when they observed the extraordinary skill employed by the players. The game was no less a startling surprise than a pleasant novelty. The spectators had never dreamed of the opportunities for brilliant scientific play, for the strategy and for quickly executed movements of mind and body."

The New York Giants had started strong by winning their first two games but an 8-1 defeat by Brooklyn was their downfall. On October 23rd, a Tuesday, when only 500 people appeared at Baltimore to watch the Orioles overwhelm Philadelphia 6-1, the fate of the league seemed clear. Other cities had been going deeper and deeper into debt, and survival had become problematical. Gates often dipped below 500 spectators.

With the heavy over-balance of strength on the Baltimore eleven, interest soon diminished in other cities. According to newspaper reports Baltimore enjoyed home crowds of 3,000 to 8,000 spectators at weekend games. It was a source of encouragement to the Baltimore officials but the other cities in the league were not so fortunate.

When Baltimore defeated 10-1 in a return game at Washington there was a decidedly negative response from the Washington press and it brought up a new problem. The *Washington Post* created quite a furore when it reported:

"Baltimore's professional football team found Washington about as easy to beat as the baseball Orioles found the Senators during the baseball season. Manager New Hanlon never does things by halves so when he went into football he worked with the same energy that characterized his work in baseball.

"To use a sporting phrase, Hanlon 'rung in a cold deck' on the other managers of the league.

"When this team lined up at National Park yesterday it was found that in its makeup were Little, Calvey, Ferguson and Wallace of the Manchester, England team, champions of Great Britain and home of the Association game. They simply toyed with Manager Schmelz' Senators."

The Washington story caused immigration officials of the United States Treasury Department to come into the act. The moot point was whether or not the federal labor laws pertaining to alien workers could be applied to professional sports activities.

Under the date line Washington, D.C., October 18, 1894 the *Boston Herald* said:

"Considerable interest is taken in treasury circles in the newspaper statement that a number of players in the Baltimore professional football team are Englishmen and prior to coming to the United States were engaged in professional football playing in England.

"In August of this year the treasury officials were asked if professional football players under contract would be allowed to land. The application came from Baltimore through a person who wished to import a complete English team to play in the United States. In answer to this request, Secretary Carlisle telegraphed as follows: 'In the opinion of the department, football players are not artists and coming into the United States under contract would be prohibited from landing.'

"Whether these players now engaged by Baltimore are part of the players who desired to come into the United States in August last is not known to the treasury department but the immigration bureau of the department will probably investigate the allegations made."

Under the heading "The Club's Side of the Story" the *Boston Herald* carried an account from Baltimore, Maryland dated October 18th.

"The officials of the Baltimore Baseball and Exhibition Company assert that they have never had any correspondence with Secretary Carlisle in relation to bringing into the United States professional football players from England or elsewhere. Nearly all the men on the Baltimore team are residents of Detroit."

The confrontation between the immigration authorities and the Baltimore club over the alleged importation of players from England, for whom the proper work visas had not been issued by the Federal Immigration Service, invoked a widespread investigation. It was a cloud that hung over the league for the duration of its season. Although the newspapers credited the Manchester City eleven with being champions of England, in reality the team was a new addition to the English League Second Division. The players in question had jumped their contracts with the newly formed English team. All the men involved were top-class professionals. The defection to America of Calvey, Ferguson, Little and Wallace created a small sensation in the British newspapers but when Fred Davies, who had already signed a contract with the famous Sheffield United club joined the group bound for the United States, it created an uproar in the British professional soccer ranks.

Actually, six days before the Baltimore-Philadelphia game and without Baltimore's knowledge, the league directors in a well kept secret session had met in New York City and decided to cease operations. The *Boston Herald* of October 21st printed a report out of New York:

> "The late period at which this association got underway and the difficulty of avoiding conflict with the regular college football games, proved a serious obstacle to carrying out a schedule of games but the association feels that with the experience that it has gained it will be in good condition to reorganize in the opening of 1895. The association will during the winter months arrange to reorganize on somewhat different lines for spring work."

Washington led by Earle Wagner and Baltimore under the leadership of Chris Vonder Horse wanted to continue the league. Wagner declared in opposing abandonment:

> "I went into the scheme with the full expectation of losing a few dollars this preliminary season, knowing that the game in time will take with the masses and we will be reimbursed for our outlay if we have a little patience. This was intended merely as a season of education."

Evidently, the owners of the other teams thought otherwise and were reluctant to invest more money in an enterprise that they should have realized would require, like any business opportunity, a reasonable period of development. It was a specious excuse at the best to declare as a failure a venture of this potential on the basis of three short weeks. Baseball, admittedly, was the basic interest of the team owners. With the limited financial capital that was available to them for professional sports promotion they did not want to jeopardize their existing investment in an already successful project by assuming the load of a new undertaking.

That the effort failed was no indictment of the game of soccer but it did prove that insufficient study and analysis of the proposition had taken place and that little or no groundwork had been done to expose and educate the sports public in general to the merits of the sport. Big league professional soccer would have to wait. The final standing of the clubs in a league that could have changed the destiny of soccer in the United States listed Baltimore in first place with an undefeated record.

American League of Professional Football Clubs — 1894

Team	Won	Lost	Points
Baltimore	6	0	12
Brooklyn	5	1	10
Boston	3	3	6
Philadelphia	3	5	6
New York	2	4	4
Washington	1	7	2

4
BOSTON SCHOOLBOYS

The marker on the Boston Common, recognizing the first organized soccer team in the United States, the Oneida Football Club. The monument was placed here in 1925 by the seven surviving members of that team.

4

The origin of soccer in its primitive stage is a matter of conjecture. Some credit the sport to the Chinese, the Romans, the Greeks, or other sources, depending upon their background. The answer is wrapped in the mythology of the past.

In the United States the first organized football team in the modern sense was the Oneida Football Club of Boston. It was formed in 1862 and ceased to operate in 1865 after three undefeated seasons during which it was unscored upon. The club was assembled in the summer of 1862 by Gerrit Smith Miller of Peterboro, N.Y. who was a pupil at the Epes Sargent Dixwell Private Latin School of Boston. Twelve players were drafted from the Dixwell School, two from Boston English High School and one from the Boston Public Latin School. The sport had developed from the playground games that were prevalent at the Boston high schools. By design, the rules were very similar to the code that was adopted by the Football Association in England during 1863.

James D'Wolf Lovett, a player on the Oneida Club in his memoirs *Old Boston Boys and the Games They Played* said, "It was a very strong club and played matches repeatedly with the Public Latin School, English High School and Dorchester High School, beating them so easily that a match was made with the combined forces of the Boston Latin and English High schools. Even this array could make no headway against us."

The *Boston Daily Advertiser* of November 9, 1863 noted the game two days after it had been played:

> "Football: An interesting game of football took place on Saturday afternoon between the well known Oneida Club and a chosen sixteen of the high and latin schools of this city. Three games were played in all of which, although severely contested, the Oneida were victorious."

Miller, himself, explained the game, "As the ball was in constant motion after the kickoff our players were placed in the field where they would be most likely to catch or meet the ball when kicked by our opponents, in order that we might return it without delay towards their goal."

The Boston Society for the Preservation of New England Antiquities in 1923 was presented with the ball that was used in the game. The society also received the uniform worn by the players, a simple but distinctive red handkerchief, that was tied around the head, Indian style. The ball itself was round with a sort of rubberized canvas cover.

In 1923 friends of Gerrit Miller unveiled a bronze tablet in his memory at the Noble and Greenough School in Dedham, Mass. This school was a successor to the earlier Dixwell school that Miller had attended. The inscription on the bronze memorial read:

IN HONOR OF
GERRIT SMITH MILLER
A MEMBER OF
EPES SARGENT DIXWELL SCHOOL — 1860-1865
FOUNDER AND CAPTAIN
OF THE ONEIDA FOOTBALL CLUB
BOSTON 1862
THE FIRST ORGANIZED FOOTBALL CLUB
IN THE UNITED STATES
— — — — — — — —

In Boston on the Common near the Spruce Street Gate a six foot six inch high monument was erected on November 21st, 1925 to commemorate the Oneida Club as the first organized football team in America. Some of the surviving members of the club and friends, including the families of the members who had passed away, felt that such a reminder would be appropriate. Winthrop Scudder, James D'Wolf Lovett, Prof. Francis G. Peabody, Dr. Robert Means Lawrence, Edward L. Arnold and Edward Bowditch, all prominent family names in Boston were seven of the original Oneidas who were present for the ceremonies. On the face of the monument this statement appeared:

"ON THIS FIELD THE ONEIDA
FOOTBALL CLUB OF BOSTON
THE FIRST ORGANIZED FOOTBALL
CLUB IN THE UNITED STATES
PLAYED AGAINST ALL COMERS
FROM 1862 TO 1865. THE ONEIDA
GOAL WAS NEVER CROSSED."

5

BRINGING PEOPLE TOGETHER
Soccer Becomes
More Than a Kickabout

Soccer had to keep its house in order in 1921, too. (The National Cup, played in Pawtucket, Rhode Island.)

5

Organized team sports in both the United States and Britain were a phenomenon of the last half of the nineteenth century. In America they came of age in the years immediately following the end of the American Civil War.

In the beginning team sports were a prerogative of the so-called "Gentlemen" athletes of the well-to-do elements of society. They were the only ones with sufficient free time and energy to participate in such competitive activities. The emerging American football of the late 1870s, college style, was almost entirely a sport for the students, and was seldom played outside of the inter-collegiate ranks.

The post war years of the 1870s and 1880s unleashed a flood of newcomers to America. Millions of people immigrated to these shores from Europe and in most cases they settled in the eastern half of the country where the booming "Industrial Revolution" provided many opportunities for work. A few intrepid souls continued westward often through wild Indian territory to the Pacific Coast. By the 1880s advancing labor legislation was beginning to create more leisure time for the working population in general.

Team games such as baseball and soccer had become the prime source of recreation for the younger men of the era. Baseball was the pastime of the native-born Americans and they played it from April until November in the populated areas of the East and Mid-West. Soccer was the sports outlet for the newly arrived immigrants from Britain and Ireland, who settled in great numbers in the mill towns, mining and steel communities, machine tool centers and shipbuilding districts. Participation in soccer by these new Americans of foreign birth was encouraged by employers as an inducement for the workers to remain in small industrial towns and villages.

For the first time the common man of limited means was acquiring an interest in recreation. Team sports were losing their status as the preserve only of the student or man of financial standing. As early as 1881 in St. Louis, Missouri, American born players were displaying enthusiasm for the game of soccer. A squad of home grown players during that year was involved in a challenge game with a team of their peers made up of Irish immigrants and were defeated by a score of 4 goals to 2.

The same decade found soccer clubs emerging in New York City and vicinity, Philadelphia, Newark, Pittsburgh, Chicago, San Francisco, Providence, Pawtucket, Fall River, Massachusetts, Boston and Manchester, N.H. as well as in a multitude of small towns and villages throughout the East and Mid-West.

It was in 1884 that the American Football Association was formed in Newark, N.J. to bring some kind of order out of the chaotic conditions that existed in soccer affairs throughout the East. The administration of the game was split among a multiple of self-centered groups with various interpretations of the rules to suit local idiosyncrasies. Cities in the Mid-West such as Chicago, St. Louis and Detroit had many of the same problems but the population centers in that section of the country were farther apart than in the East.

The American Football Association was a loosely knit organization that provided uniform rule interpretations and an annual Cup competition that encompassed the entire eastern soccer complex. Although the individual sectional leagues and associations maintained their autonomy, the American Football Association laid the groundwork for an eventual national governing structure. It helped the growth of soccer until 1899 when a series of circumstances brought its activities to a halt. With the general labor unrest in Fall River and other mill areas following the depression of the early years of the decade, thousands of workers were unemployed. Conditions made it impossible for the New England clubs to function. In New York, New Jersey and Pennsylvania professionalism was creating havoc among the established clubs and their players. The predatory tactics of many teams in acquiring players for their rosters had set asunder the best laid plans for an orderly and efficient operation.

It was not until 1906 that the American Football Association rose again from the ashes of disillusionment. The visits of touring teams from England had stimulated a new interest in the game of soccer countrywide and many new clubs were springing up. The revival of college soccer with the formation of the Inter-collegiate Association also helped to disseminate enthusiasm for the sport. The American Football Association with its open cup competition had once again produced a force with the potential for national jurisdiction over the game. Originally, the association had an amateur orientation but with its rebirth it also became a voice for the professional interests of the East.

Over the years the American Football Association developed an informal alliance with the British Associations of England and Scotland rather than with the recently organized international FIFA confederation. This deference of the association to the British soccer powers hit a sour note with many American soccer people who felt that the United States national body should be entirely devoid of ties with any other particular country except where the mutual interests of both were concerned.

The American Football Association, despite its concern with soccer in the East, displayed very little interest in national expansion. This conservative attitude led to a growing feeling among rival soccer groups that there was room for a more progressive and imaginative administration to govern soccer on a nationwide basis.

It was upon this premise that the American Amateur Football Association took root under the guidance of the New York State Association, which had remained aloof from the American Football Association. Thomas Cahill, an American-born sports executive from St. Louis, who was secretary of the New York Association and Thomas Bagnall, President of the New York group, had decided to set up a federation that could command allegiance from the national and international elements of the game.

Dr. G. Randolph Manning of New York was elected to the Presidency of the new American Amateur Football Association at its annual general meeting in New York City on September 5, 1912. Thomas Cahill was elected secretary at the same time. Dr. Manning was born in England but was educated in Germany. While pursuing his medical studies at Heidelberg University he played soccer and soon became involved in the administrative affairs of German soccer. He became a prime mover in the formation of the German Football Association in 1904 and helped it to obtain FIFA recognition.

Later he immigrated to the United States to assume the practice of medicine in New York City.

With international soccer in his background, he soon advocated membership in the Federation International de Football Association (FIFA) for the American Amateur Football Association. It was at his suggestion that Thomas Cahill was sent as a representative of the American Association to the Ninth Annual Congress of FIFA at Stockholm, Sweden on June 30, and July 1, 1912 for the purpose of gaining membership in the international body.

The American Football Association was seeking an affiliation of its own with FIFA and was unaware of Cahill's presence at the congress until advised by its British contacts. Fearing a "faite accompli" by the amateur forces, the American Football Association requested F. J. Wall, secretary of the Football Association of England, to present its case. The proposal on behalf of the American Amateur Football Association was put forward by Thomas Cahill but it was opposed by F. J. Wall, who based his objections on the fact that the American Amateur Football Association did not control the professional and amateur groups in the United States. He maintained that FIFA should not become a clearing house for the internal problems of soccer in the United States. He suggested that Cahill should be advised to return to America and to help bring the warring factions into a single union. FIFA urged the acceptance of an American affiliate at the proper time under the proper circumstances. It produced a stalemate in the plans of the rival American associations.

The rebuff by FIFA did not deter the objective of Cahill and his associates. Upon his return to the United States a committee of Cahill, William Campbell and N. Ager, all of New York City, was appointed to meet with a similar committee from the American Football Association. As a result of this session, negotiations for common front appeared to be progressing favorably but on December 8, 1912 the American Football Association announced that its "peace" committee had been discharged by a 7-6 vote. This setback brought a halt to the plans for an amalgamation of the two associations.

Dr. Manning and Thomas Cahill decided to seek the cooperation of the Allied American Football Association of Philadelphia, one of the largest and best governed bodies in the country not yet committed to either side, in an effort to create a really national federation. At a private meeting in New York City on March 8, 1913 the Allied American representatives agreed to assist the American Amateur Football Association in the formation of a nationwide organization.

The Astor House in New York City became the rally point on April 5th for soccer minded people from all parts of the United States. The meeting became the first soccer convention of national scope to be held in the nation. From this session came the name of a new organization, the United States of America Football Association.

On the 21st of June the by-laws and rules of procedure were passed and a set of officers was elected with Dr. Manning as President.

After the April 5th meeting a new application for recognition had been forwarded to FIFA on behalf of the new United States of America Football Association. As the organization of the U.S.A.F.A. was not completed until after the FIFA meeting in Copenhagen, the application received at Copenhagen was turned over to the Emergency Committee with instructions to give provisional recognition to the United States of America Football Association when a permanent organization had been set up.

Despite this assurance by August 13th speculation was rampant as to which group had been accepted by FIFA. The National Football League, the nucleus of the American Football Association, had agreed earlier in the month to join the United States Association, provided international acceptance was forthcoming. On August 9th the American Football Association met again to consider an alliance with the United States Football Association but the vote was negative again by a 5-4 ballot.

It was an eventful day for American soccer on Friday, August 15, 1913, when a cablegram from Europe advised the United States of America Football Association that it had been granted provisional membership. The next day the American Football Association by a vote of 10 to 2 decided to rescind its decision of the previous week and submit to the authority of the new national association. The soccer organizers had ended their long power struggle.

UNITED STATES OF AMERICA FOOTBALL ASSOCIATION
1913-1914

Affiliated:
    Allied Amateur Cup Competition, Philadelphia
    American Football Association, Newark, New Jersey
    Associated Football League, Chicago, Illinois
    Cleveland Association Football League, Cleveland, Ohio
    Michigan State Association Football League, Detroit, Michigan
    National Association Football League, Newark, New Jersey
    New Jersey Amateur Football League, Newark, New Jersey
    Peel Challenge Cup Commission, Chicago, Illinois
    No. Massachusetts and So. New Hampshire State Soccer Football
        Association, Boston, Massachusetts
    So. New England Football Association, Providence, Rhode Island
    Southern New York State Football Association
    St. Louis Soccer Football League, St. Louis, Missouri
    The Football Association of Eastern Pennsylvania, Philadelphia, Pa.
    Utah Association Football Union, Salt Lake City, Utah
    Western Pennsylvania Football Association, Pittsburgh, Pennsylvania

A Corinthians player prepares to receive a pass, as they tied Fore River, of Quincy, Massachusetts, 1-1. The date was September 14, 1906 at the Locust Street, Boston National League baseball grounds.

6
THE AMATEURS
Playing for Fun

The American Soccer Champion in 1883, 1884, and 1885, Clark's O.N.T. team.

This team of Massachusetts All-Stars travelled to New Brunswick in Canada for friendly games. It was just following the Depression, and the game was floundering in America.

6

"Somehow we occasionally get away from the purpose of amateur sports, which is to play. It is not a business."

Prior to the founding of the United States Soccer Federation in 1913 the distinction between amateur and professional players was nebulous. The only authority of long standing at that time was the American Football Association, which professed to oversee the professional phase of the game in the East. The nucleus of its control was the National League of New Jersey, which actually was a semi-professional group of part-timers, and the American Cup Competition which provided limited supervision over individually motivated entries from several eastern states.

In soccer, unlike many other team sports, it was not easy to diagnose the difference between an amateur and a professional club. With players able to compete with or against each other, defining an amateur or a professional club proved impossible. The pseudo-amateur player was often as well reimbursed for his services as was his professional counterpart.

Many of the soccer clubs were ethnic in their origin but in cities such as St. Louis, Newark, Philadelphia, Pittsburgh and Fall River, second generation Americans and their native-born friends also were making substantial contributions to the bumper crop of new soccer teams. Surprisingly, few of the clubs used ethnic names. In most cases the amateur clubs represented the employees of industrial corporations or took the names of community sponsors. In fact the "ethnic" naming of teams was a product of the post World War Two era.

The amateur administrators were quick to realize that the improved means of transportation that had developed after the turn of the century through the rapid expansion of steam and electric railway facilities had broadened the perimeters of the game. It had made interstate and inter-city travel and competition both feasible and attractive in the same way that air travel in 1946 had provided new horizons and made transcontinental and international competition a reality.

The inauguration of the National Open Cup Competition in 1914 by the United States Soccer Football Association provided a long overdue opportunity for clubs from all sections of the country to test their strength in interstate competitive play. Without a clearly defined amateur competition, the amateurs were still able to compete effectively, while pure professionalism was relatively indistinct.

It was not until the organization of the American Professional Soccer League in 1921 that a new dilemma was presented to amateur clubs and their followers in their quest for national honors.

The new American Professional League, the St. Louis Professional League and the well financed sectional and industrially sponsored semi-professional leagues had become the dominant forces in the National Open Cup Competition. To accommodate the needs of the amateurs, the United States Football Association instituted the National Amateur Cup Competition in 1923. It is interesting to note that many teams with American-born players dominated this tournament.

The Olympic Games of 1924 provided an opportunity for the United States Soccer Football Association to make its first serious appearance in world amateur soccer. Previously, the United States in 1904 and before the formation of the national association had participated in a disappointing Olympic program against Canada. In 1924 a representative squad of American-born players and Americans of foreign birth won the first round game with Estonia 1-0. In the second round the American team met Uruguay, the eventual champions, and were defeated 3-0. The American team made a disappointing appearance at the 1928 Antwerp Olympic Games and was badly beaten 11-2 by Italy in the first round.

The failure to include soccer on the Olympic schedule for the 1932 games at Los Angeles was a set-back for the progress of the game in the United States. Amateur soccer in America was at a high standard during this era, with thousands of fine American players available. The presence of an Olympic soccer tournament on American soil would have given tremendous prestige to the sport in this country and it would have helped its image immeasurably with the average American.

The United States displayed unsuspected strength in the Olympic Games of 1936 at Berlin, Germany. The Italian team that eventually won the Gold medal managed to eliminate the American team in the first round of the tournament by a close 1 to 0 score. Once again the United States was drawn against the cream of the crop at the beginning of the competition. Fourteen players from an American squad of seventeen were native born.

Many quality American-born players were being developed even in the years before 1950. These players usually were products of the urban sand-lots, where they perfected their skills by playing with and against new-comers from Britain, Europe and South America.

In subsequent Olympic competitions the American teams were never in close contention with the better teams of Europe and South America. In 1948 at London, 1952 at Helsinki and 1956 in Australia the United States teams were outclassed. With the introduction of the preliminary qualifying rounds in 1960 for providing an ultimate sixteen teams for the final Olympic series, it seemed to be an ideal formula by which the United States could continue to progress. In 1972 at Munich the American team survived the qualifying rounds. Unfortunately a strong West German club overcame the United States eleven by a 7 to 0 score with goalkeeper Shep Messing making 62 saves!

The explosive development of homebred talent in the youth move-ments of the 1960s marked a step forward in the progress of soccer.

Many promising players have joined the existing senior amateur clubs and have been involved in competition with and against Americans of foreign birth. It has been a process that in times past has provided the crucible from which many great native-born players have emerged. Unfor-tunately, the expanding intercollegiate soccer front with its availability of scholarships and the lure of the Professional League college draft has brought about a bypass of traditional club environment.

The unparalleled expansion of summer soccer recreational facili-ties for competitive play during the twilight hours of the day has con-tributed to a trend. The summer programs are less rigid but more self-disciplined than the league play of the ethnic oriented teams under the jurisdiction of the United States Soccer Federation during the traditional Fall, Winter and Spring seasons. Yet it is in this phase of amateur senior soccer that the greatest gains have been made in recent years. Although these soccer programs have been largely devoid of United States Soccer Federation influence, they have represented the acceptance by municipal recreational authorities of the spreading soccer dogma.

The American Youth Soccer organization which entered the field of youth soccer promotion in 1964 has been a dominant force in exploring and developing the mass enrollment of boys and girls into the future of American soccer. The United States Soccer Federation, inspired by the AYSO approach, reconstructed its own youth program into an efficient and effective medium for soccer progress. Both of these movements have made sufficient contributions to homebred soccer in their own individual ways.

As Dr. G. Randolph Manning of New York, the first president of the
United States Soccer Federation so aptly and prophetically put it in 1929
at a lecture under the auspices of the General George W. Wingate Memorial
Fund, "We are not so much interested in the development of star teams or
super champions — this phase takes care of itself in the ordinary run of
events — but we place all our efforts in gaining the support and active
attendance of tens of thousands of our youth, who would otherwise stand
on the sidelines as a cheering but non-active entity."

The development efforts of the United States Soccer Federation
during the traumatic years of the nineteen-sixties and seventies have been
centered on youth activities and the professional evolution. All of these
objectives are worthy of consideration but they are only part of the picture. Little credence has been given to the durable contributions of the
senior amateur club both in the past and present decades. Yet it is well to
remember that since the formation of the United States Federation in
1913 the strength and the backbone of American soccer has been the
amateur senior club eleven. The game may someday acknowledge this
senior amateur club status.

*Many amateur leagues were, and are, played in relative obscurity, with limited interest from
outsiders. This game took place in 1908. Note the referee's clothing (left).*

7
RISING AND FALLING
WITH THE PROFESSIONALS
Soccer Almost Defeats Itself

The game was hard, the contact frequent, and players paid little attention to the field conditions.

Quality soccer players in America were both native and foreign-born. The Boston Wonder Workers 1927 team boasted 10 former Scottish players, including two who had played on the Scottish National Team.

7

Professional soccer has enjoyed a long but varied existence during its history. Contrary to popular belief, professional soccer is not a new phenomenon in American sports. Of all the team games in the United States, only baseball can boast of an earlier appearance on the professional scene.

The abundance of immigration from Britain and Ireland during the eighteen-eighties accelerated the growth of soccer in America and brought about the formation of the American Football Association at Newark, N.J. in 1884. Before that date, except for an abortive attempt by the eastern colleges in the eighteen-seventies to popularize the game, soccer was a spasmodic and poorly organized activity and played almost exclusively by the working people of the manufacturing and industrial areas.

It was not until 1888 that professionalism came of age in England with the organization of the English League, long after professional baseball in the United States had reached the same stage. The decision of the Football Association of England to recognize the professional element in 1885 had laid the groundwork for a professional league venture. It was an historic moment for the sport after years of controversy and it elevated professional soccer to a stable and respected position in the athletic world.

Amateur soccer towards the end of the nineteenth century had become a recreational outlet for most immigrants from Britain and Ireland in America. Neo-professionalism did exist among some clubs that were able to provide jobs or liberal expense money as an inducement to attract players. The first hint of real professional activity among American soccer men did not occur until 1891, when a Canadian All-star team made a second visit to the British Isles.

Several American players were with the Canadian squad on this tour. The team played a busy schedule of fifty games over a period ranging from August 1891 until January 1892. The competition was furnished by professional league teams and international elevens from England,

Scotland, Ireland and Wales. At the conclusion of this lengthy jaunt several of the players were persuaded to remain in England and join English League clubs. The remainder of the squad returned to America, their families, and their jobs.

In the United States soccer was having its growing pains as more and more soccer minded newcomers came to these shores from abroad. It was in 1894, only six years after professional league soccer emerged in Britain, that the American League of Professional Football (Soccer) Clubs came into existence along the Eastern Seaboard. It was a poorly conceived plan, but did introduce professional soccer to the United States on a major league level.

The failure of the major league baseball owners to make a success of professional soccer in 1894 (see Chapter 3) had a distressing effect on others who might have been tempted to promote the professional game. Plans were in the works for a professional league made up of the better clubs in the American Football (Soccer) Association in the later eighteen-nineties but unfortunately the Spanish-American War of 1898, the general labor unrest in New England and other mill districts, which found thousands of men out of work, restrained their enthusiasm. In fact the war and labor strife had a depressing effect on the entire soccer scene and stymied the progress of the American Football Association. The American Cup Competition, emblematic of the national soccer championship, was abandoned from 1899 to 1906.

At The Turn of The Century

In 1901 plans were made to create a professional soccer league in the Mid-west with teams from St. Louis, Chicago, Detroit and Milwaukee. Charles Comiskey of the Chicago White Sox and other major league baseball men from other mid-western cities re-entered the scene, but the necessary financial support failed to materialize.

The visits of the Pilgrim and the Corinthians All-star teams from England to the United States and Canada during the first decade of the twentieth century brought a taste of the best soccer in the world to American sports followers. These touring contingents were instrumental in igniting the fires that brought about the resurrection of soccer in 1905 as part of the sports curriculum in our American schools and colleges, an area where the game had been relatively dormant since 1876. Hopes were renewed again that soccer would eventually be nurtured into a great collegiate pastime to complement the growth of the game in amateur club circles, particularly among the foreign born element of the population.

Until the organization of the American Soccer League in 1921 organizations such as the National League in the Middle Atlantic States of New York, New Jersey and Pennsylvania, the Southern New England League of Massachusetts and Rhode Island and the St. Louis League provided the most visible form of professional soccer in the United States. None of the players were full-time professionals, however.

These leagues of semi-professional teams prospered in the larger industrial and commercial areas, where soccer was "in the air." The players often received compensation for their services, equalling the wages of professional league players in Britain. Many American teams, sponsored by industrial organizations in the East, offered financial advantages in the way of high salaries and extra remuneration for playing soccer. Professionalism on a part-time basis was strong in the American soccer areas of St. Louis, New England, Northern New Jersey, Eastern and Western Pennsylvania, New York City, Chicago and Detroit.

There were many outstanding players in this era, including men such as Billy Gillespie, Stanley Fazackerly, Mick King, Tom Murray, Jock Ferguson, Tom Hislop, Ben Gouvier and Whitey Fleming from the English and Scottish professional leagues and American born and bred players such as Davie Brown, Archie Stark, Fred Lennox, Harry Ratican, Bull Brannigan, Harry Marre, Jimmy Easton, Tommy Swords, Sinky Sullivan, Frank Burnes of Fall River, Jim Spalding, Jim Wilson of Philadelphia and Pete Renzulli of New York.

A Professional League

The plan to initiate a new professional league, that could become the basis for a full-time professional group, unfolded at the meeting that was held in Newark in September 1909 with delegates from the soccer centers of the East to promote an Eastern Professional League. The strongest teams along the Atlantic Coast were represented at this session. Six teams from Fall River, Pawtucket, Philadelphia (Hibernians), Philadelphia (Thistle), Newark and Harrison (New Jersey) affiliated with the organization.

Andrew M. Brown, later to become president of the United States Football Association, and Tom Adams, a long time professional advocate, were prime movers in the league. The league survived one year with an abbreviated schedule that found the Fall River Rovers in first place when the league season came to an abrupt ending. Although the attendance at the games was as expected, the inclement weather contributed insurmountable schedule difficulties that spelled an early demise for this ambitious effort.

The Eastern League was succeeded by the National League, which prospered until 1921. In order to reduce traveling expense this league restricted its roster of clubs to the states of New York, New Jersey and Pennsylvania. The New England teams in turn organized their own sectional league.

In the second decade of this century the first great American professional soccer team emerged at Bethlehem, Pennsylvania. Under the name of the Bethlehem Steel F.C. it epitomized the ultimate in American professional soccer. In an era when professional baseball and collegiate football represented the acme of team sports, the charisma that surrounded this soccer power was amazing. The success of the club was assured, as the upper hierarchy of the Bethlehem Steel Company had taken a paternal interest in the venture. Herbert Lewis, executive vice president of the company recruited the best professional talent available in the British Isles to augment a number of fine American players.

The war in Europe from 1914 to 1918 had a depressing effect on American soccer, as it did on the whole of American life. The end of hostilities in 1918, however, released new waves of immigrants to these shores and by the early 1920s the time was ripe for another approach towards a major professional soccer league.

When Sports Were Golden

At the beginning of the "Golden Age of Sport" in America, with heroes such as Red Grange, Babe Ruth, and Jack Dempsey, the American Soccer League with an eight team group of clubs in five Eastern states, began operations. A regular schedule of games to be played on Saturdays, Sundays and holidays was formulated.

Actually, it was the semi-professional leagues of the Eastern States that had paved the way for the effort to create a truly successful professional soccer organization. Fortunately for American professional soccer the British Association had withdrawn from FIFA in 1920 and it was not until 1924 that they returned to the International fold. In the interim many prominent players from the British Isles migrated to the United States to join the newly established American Soccer League. Within a short time more players of ability from the soccer-oriented countries of Continental Europe became a part of the mass movement of soccer talent to America.

The clubs franchised by the league in the important soccer centers of the East were Philadelphia, Jersey City, Pawtucket, Fall River, Harrison, Holyoke, New York and Brooklyn. It was a full-time professional enterprise with the players registered on professional contracts.

Originally the league planned to include Bethlehem Steel, three times national champion, on its roster of clubs but it was necessary at the last moment to replace the Bethlehem eleven with the Falcos from Holyoke. The majority of the Bethlehem Steel players joined the Philadelphia entry.

The American Soccer League owed its existence to Thomas W. Cahill of St. Louis and New York, a native-born soccer devotee, who had been the executive secretary for the United States Soccer Football Association from its inception in 1913. It had been Cahill's dream to place soccer on a plane in the United States comparable with its standing in Britain and Europe and to establish it as the national pastime for the Fall, Winter and Spring months.

A strong competitor, the National Professional Football (American) league had been formed the year earlier in 1920 with a composition of clubs that resembled the make-up of the soccer venture. Industrial teams and newly organized professional clubs were included in the roster of the National League. Both the American Soccer League and the National Football League were invading the professional sports arena, where professional baseball had enjoyed a private sanctuary for more than seventy-five years.

The nineteen twenties were an epoch in the history of American soccer as many of the finest players in the world appeared in the line-ups of American soccer League teams for almost a decade. Writeups on individual players and teams appeared in large print on the sports pages of the larger metropolitan daily newspapers for the first time to provide a backlog of soccer folklore for future generations. It was a period when many great American born and American developed players attained international status. Players such as Bill Gonsalves, Barney Battles, John Nilson of Boston, Tom Florie of Providence, Arnie Oliver of New Bedford, Bert Patenaude of Fall River, Pete Renzulli of New York, Archie Stark and Davie Brown of Newark became world class. This period was called the "Renaissance of American Soccer." One of the leading writers of the time said, "We really didn't think too much about European soccer then. The best soccer being played anywhere was right here in America."

Many other players emerged as proficient professionals in America, after coming here as teenagers. Some of them such as Alec Jackson and Battles returned overseas eventually to represent their native countries in international competition. Andy Muirhead, a Scottish international, came to the United States as player-manager of the Boston team and returned home after a few years to again reach international status. Later he became manager of Glasgow Rangers.

Alec Jackson played in both the Scottish and English Leagues after his American sojourn and in 1928 tallied three goals for "Wembley Wizards" of Scotland against England in one of the great international games of all time at Wembley Stadium, London. Barney Battles, son of a famous

Scottish player, played in the local Boston and District League at seventeen and graduated to the Boston Wonder Workers of the American League where he became a leading player. He, too, went back to Scotland to achieve international fame. It was a period when American soccer was of World class and the incubator of many international greats.

The American Soccer League made an auspicious start in the fall of 1921 and until the 1924-1925 season remained an eight club organization. By that time Bethlehem Steel had become a member of the league. The New York club had been acquired by the Indiana Flooring interests of New York. Falcos of Holyoke, Massachusetts, Todd Shipyards of Brooklyn and Jersey City had passed into oblivion but the National Giants of New York, Fall River, Massachusetts and Newark had been awarded franchises.

The 1924-1925 season heralded a new forward movement by the league. Boston, Providence, Fleischer Yarn of Philadelphia and New Bedford were added to the league roster, making a 12 team league. The advent of Boston with a veteran cast of players from the premier divisions of the English and Scottish Leagues brought professional American soccer a step nearer to acceptance as a major American sport after years of rebuff. Players of the caliber of Andy Muirhead, Mickey Hamil, Tom McMillan, Jock McIntyre and Alec MacNabb, all international players, gave the team a formidable front. Other clubs in the league had also benefitted from the acquisition of first class English and Scottish talent during the absence of the British Associations from FIFA.

The expansion plan opened the floodgates for seasoned British and European players to immigrate to the United States for the opportunity to accept the generous financial inducements that were being offered by American Soccer League teams.

Leadership Is Lacking

By 1926 dissatisfaction was simmering between the amateur and professional factions of the United States Soccer Football Association, but the threat of a split between the rival forces did not erupt until the fall of 1928. By this time the American Soccer League had emulated professional baseball by appointing a National Commissioner. Bill Cunningham, a national sports columnist from the *Boston Morning Post*, was selected for the position. Cunningham, originally from Texas, had been an All-American football selection while at Dartmouth College and was a respected influence in professional and intercollegiate football. It was an attempt to secure additional recognition from the news media by emphasizing soccer's universal appeal. Although there was some merit to this move, it was unfortunate that a man more familiar with soccer and its nuances was not at the helm during this troubled period for the game.

When trouble brewed at the Helsinki Congress of FIFA in 1927 and the U.S.S.F.A. was threatened with expulsion for harboring and playing foreign professional players who had abrogated their contracts overseas, it was only through the good offices and diplomacy of Andrew M. Brown, the U.S.S.F.A. president, that trouble was averted.

A major problem arose when soccer factions had differences over National Open Cup Competition. The management of the league felt that Cup obligations interfered with the continuity of the American league schedule. Accordingly, the league voted to have the clubs abstain from taking part in the National Cup Competition.

When the New York Giants, Bethlehem Steel and Newark teams defied the league edict and entered the national competition, they were suspended by the league. The U.S.S.F.A. failed to recognize this dictum and refused to declare the clubs ineligible.

The teams suspended by the American Soccer League remained in good standing with the United States Football Association and organized a new professional league known as the Eastern Professional League. Bethlehem Steel, Newark, New York Giants, New York Hispano, New York Hungaria, New York Hakoah, I.R.T. Rangers, and the Newark Portuguese became members of the new group.

The Southern New York Association claimed that its territorial rights had been invaded by this action and withdrew from the United States Football Association. There was some talk that a rival national association would be formed to challenge the U.S.F.A., but it never materialized.

An attempt was made by groups who supported the American Soccer League position to interest other Eastern state associations in their cause. They invited representatives to a meeting in New York City but there was a negative response to the endeavor. The so-called "outlaws" represented by the American League and the Southern New York Association felt that they would be able to arrange international games with the British Associations, which at this time were not affiliated with FIFA. They received no encouragement.

As a result of the ultimatum issued by the American Soccer League, the United States Soccer Football Association withdrew its approval of the professional franchise and suspended the organization. All clubs that failed to sever their affiliation with the American League were subject to the same sanctions.

The American Soccer League and the Eastern Professional League began a struggle for the support of the soccer populace to their mutual disadvantage until Thomas Cahill, secretary of the U.S.S.F.A. was successful in negotiating a peace settlement on October 9, 1929. The wounds of battle remained to scar the American professional scene for many years. Many influential and wealthy men such as H. E. Lewis of Bethlehem Steel Company and G.A.G. Wood of American Woolen Company became disillusioned with the soccer situation and withdrew from the picture.

Among the discouraging aspects of the professional movement was the lack of harmony and cooperation between the American Soccer League and the United States Soccer Football Association.

It was the perfect example of the problems that can arise, when two diverse elements with the same objectives but with different approaches strive to make progress. The American League schedule carried through the winter months and in most cases it was impossible to provide adequate facilities for spectator comfort in the frigid weather. Some fields such as the Polo Grounds in New York City had covered stands that furnished some shelter in inclement weather but usually open stadium conditions existed.

A constant source of controversy between the professionals and the national ruling body was participation in the National Open Cup Competition. The U.S.S.F.A. felt that the professional league clubs owed an obligation to soccer that required their presence in the national championship series. The American League disputed this contention and deplored the interruptions in the league schedule that occurred, when teams took part in an elimination cup-tie type of play. Ironically, the American League promoted a cup-tie elimination series of its own during the league season. A power struggle for the control of American soccer was an underlying cause for discord.

The American Soccer League prospered for almost a decade but dissension, the impending depression of the "thirties," a lack of sufficient foresight and a modicum of imagination spelled the end of a period of transition during which the United States seemed to be emerging as a major world soccer power.

When the American League faltered in the early thirties, it was succeeded by a reorganized American League on a very modest scale in 1933. The major branch of the league covered a limited area from New York City to Baltimore to accommodate the financial stresses of the Great Depression. In New England various attempts were made to provide a stable adjunct to the Middle Atlantic States mainstream but its path was far from smooth.

8

FOREIGN TEAMS
VISIT AMERICA
Their Impact

The "Wonder Team of England," Charlton Athletic, visits the United States in 1937. Twenty-three thousand fans came out to see the American League All-Stars compete against the best in Europe.

8

During the 1880s and 1890s soccer in the United States appeared to be on the upgrade. At the turn of the century, however, labor unrest, a depression and the Spanish American War had served to dampen the soccer spirit. Following this period of stagnation, the first decade of the twentieth century brought about a revival of interest on a widespread basis.

The first tour of the Pilgrim F.C. from England in 1905 through Eastern Canada and the United States gave a tremendous impetus to American soccer. It also revealed the need for a national organization to bring together all elements of the game. The interest stirred up by the visitors had a very favorable impact on the news media, which gave cognizance to a sport that had been played for years in the United States by a large but relatively inarticulate group of immigrant Americans, their offspring and their families.

The Pilgrims' arrival in the United States came at an opportune time, when American college football with its mayhem and violence had incurred the wrath of an important segment of American educators and was fighting for survival.

Subsequent visits by the Corinthians from England in 1906 and 1911 and the Pilgrims again in 1909 brought a more cohesive feeling to American soccer and led to the formation of the United States Football Association (United States Soccer Federation) in 1913.

After 1920 the presence of touring professional teams from overseas became commonplace on American soil and provided a tape measure by which the playing prowess of homebred players and the progress of the American game could be gauged. The arrival of a strengthened Third Lanark F.C. from Glasgow, Scotland in 1921 set off an invasion of the United States by many teams from Britain and the continent of Europe until war broke out overseas in the late nineteen-thirties. After World War Two it was the English team, Liverpool F.C. that launched the avalanche of clubs from all corners of the earth to America. It was a movement that had a lasting effect on soccer in the United States.

This influx of soccer talent from abroad gave American soccer devotees an unequalled opportunity to observe and assess the game at its best and in all its phases. It played an important part in the ascendency of American professional soccer into major status worldwide.

As early as 1919, American teams were going abroad to test their skills. The Bethlehem Steel team toured Sweden following their National Championship win in America.

9
THE REAL
INTERNATIONAL BEGINNING
The Eighth Olympiad

The United States ventured into world soccer, following its recognition by FIFA. Here, the Estonian goalkeeper saves against the United States (in white).

The U.S. 1924 Olympic Team poses outside their hotel. Back row: Davis, Rudd, Peel (U.S.S.F. Pres.), Douglas, Jones, Hornberger, O'Connor, Collins (coach). Front row: Burford (trainer), Findley, Brix, Straden, Farrell, Dalrymple.

9

The United States made its formal debut in international soccer competition during the Olympic Games in 1924 in Paris, France.

It was a dream that had become a reality. Shortly after the formation of the United States Soccer Federation in 1913, plans had been prepared to participate in the 1916 Olympic Games at Berlin, Germany. World War I, however, intervened to cancel out the tournament. The 1920 Games were passed over by the United States Soccer Federation but progress was being made for an appearance at the Eighth Olympiad in 1924 at Paris.

George Mathew Collins of Boston, an avid soccer man and Soccer Editor of the *Boston Daily Globe*, was appointed manager and coach of the Olympic squad. After receiving a broken leg in a game one year, Collins' enthusiasm remained unabated. He continued in the game for another five years under the name of George Mathews in order to relieve his wife of any anxiety over his participation in the sport as a player.

The team sailed May 10th from New York on the S.S. America. The squad engaged in two training sessions a day, morning and afternoon aboard ship. Calisthenics and gym work occupied the morning sessions while heading, trapping, shooting and jogging filled in the afternoon program.

On arrival at Cherbourg, France on May 19th the team almost immediately entrained for Paris and the Colombes Olympic Village, adjoining the stadium. The group was met by Peter Peel, President of the United States Soccer Federation. The players were dissatisfied with their food and living quarters, which were infested. After a sleepless night, arrangements were made to house the team at a hotel thirty minutes from the center of Paris.

Estonia was the first round opponent on May 25th and proved to be a worthy foe. Andy Straden scored the only goal of the game on a penalty kick. The Estonian eleven tried hard to equalize but Douglas in the American goal was unbeatable. In the second half Estonia was awarded a penalty kick but Kajot put the ball over the crossbar and the Americans heaved a sigh of relief. It was short lived, however, as the referee ordered the kick retaken, claiming he had not blown his whistle. On the second chance Kajot hit the crossbar but Douglas gathered in the rebound and relieved the pressure. The French fans were very partisan towards the Estonians and greeted the United States team with boos, hisses, whistling, and a duck-like noise.

On June 1st the American team watched their second round opposition, Uruguay crush France 5-1 with an impressive display at Colombes Stadium. Misfortune struck the United States eleven when two regulars were unable to play against Uruguay. Dr. Brix, a clever forward, was badly injured near the end of the Estonia game and suffered a punctured kidney. Rudd at fullback was incapacitated by a bad ankle injury incurred during practice.

The contest with Uruguay at Stade Bergeyre on June 5th before 20,000 fans was a real test for the Americans. Although the United States fought hard and missed several chances at goal the Uruguay combination displayed splendid soccer and tallied three goals by Petrone before half time.

In the second half, Coach Collins made a strategic move that upstaged by a quarter of a century the Swiss "Verrou" and the Italian "Catenaccio" systems.

In an effort to hold the clever Uruguay attack in check, Collins introduced the sweeper behind a line of four backs. This move upset the rhythm of the South Americans and dulled their offensive moves for the balance of the game. Uruguay won the game 3-0 and the United States was eliminated from further competition. Ironically, after this game the French crowd cheered the American effort.

The United States played in two post-tournament contests before departing for home. On June 10th the United States defeated Poland 3-2 at Warsaw before an enthusiastic and friendly crowd. The visitors were given a wonderful reception after the game. Straden scored twice and Wells once for the Americans.

At Dublin on June 14th it was a different story as the Irish Free State eleven defeated the United States 3-1, with Hart scoring the only American goal.

As Coach George Collins reported to the United States Soccer Federation, the American team made a remarkable showing in view of the conditions involved. Most of the clubs in the Olympic Competition had been playing together for a year or two with subsidized "amateur" players. Uruguay had maintained the same squad for four years and played eleven games in Europe prior to the opening of the tournament. Uruguay was easily the best team in the competition and deserved their championship medals.

10
PROFESSIONAL SOCCER
STRUGGLES . . .
and Struggles

American Soccer League action, 1926 at Walpole Street Grounds, Boston, former home of the Boston Braves National League Baseball Team. This game was played in January. Note the bandages on players' knees to protect them from the frozen ground.

10

A new American Soccer League, completely divorced from the old group, was organized for the 1933-1934 season. The old league had been a pretentious effort to promote American professional soccer on a big time basis with top class professional players. It was a time of disturbing influences with a worldwide depression in the offing. The recreated American Soccer League, in an economy-minded world, was reluctant to expand beyond the narrow corridor between New York City and Baltimore.

Having survived the "Depression years" and later wartime restrictions, the parent American Soccer League of the Mid-Atlantic States approached the post-war era with optimism. From 1946 until the nineteen-seventies the league by itself or in conjunction with the United States Soccer Football Association underwrote the American visits of many teams from such countries as England, Scotland, Ireland, Iceland, Portugal, Germany, Israel, Mexico, Cuba, Poland, Turkey, Italy, Austria, Bermuda, Czechoslovakia, Canada, Brazil and Switzerland. In return American Soccer League teams visited Mexico, Cuba, Israel and Central and South America.

The tours of these foreign visitors were in general very successful gate attractions. The money raised from the games helped both the United States Soccer Football Association and the American Soccer League to maintain their financial stability. Crowds of 20,000 or more were common at these games. Apart from the commercial aspects of the tours they had a very positive effect on the progress of soccer in the United States. American soccer players benefited from playing against the teams from abroad and the soccer public was able to watch the best of talent from all parts of the world. The games gave American teams an opportunity to test their ability against strong foreign teams and to assess their own strength in world soccer. The league also conducted the Lewis Cup Competition for its members.

These foreign attractions set new attendance records at Yankee Stadium, the old Polo Grounds and Randalls Island Stadium in New York City and at Ebbets Field in Brooklyn.

On June 15, 1948 at Ebbets Field, the first game between two visiting professional teams from abroad played under the floodlights took place when Liverpool of England defeated Djurgarten of Sweden 3-2.

In 1958 at Randalls Island, Liverpool and Nuremburg played before 23,000 fans. During the summer of 1965 the American Soccer League staged three well patronized events. In June A. C. Milan and Santos played at Randalls Island with 25,000 people present. In August, Santos and Benfica attracted 30,000 spectators to Randalls Island and in September Santos and Inter-Milan drew 41,598 soccer followers to Yankee Stadium. It was Pele's first visit to the United States.

The American Soccer League was successful in having some of its league games televised in October 1952 at Yankee Stadium in New York but it was a short-lived experience. Another experiment included indoor soccer, which was introduced at Madison Square Garden in New York City in the winter months of 1939, 1940 and 1950. The indoor game still strives for national recognition.

The American Soccer League in the post-war period experienced both progress and setbacks in its existence, but it managed to survive through many trying years by adroit management of league affairs. It was always the visiting professional teams, however, which brought in the money, but their influence ended with the final whistle.

Even during the 1960 International Soccer Tournament, New York, the American Soccer League continued to survive like a hardy perennial. During the fall of 1964 the league had become disillusioned with its association with the International Tournament in New York and was looking for other outlets to enlist its energy. Both the American Soccer League and the German-American Soccer League were concerned with the development of major league professional soccer. The two leagues decided to cooperate in the establishment of an Eastern Professional Soccer Conference for the 1964-1965 season. The better teams from both leagues formed a twelve team organization. It was a bold experiment to test the feasibility of promoting eventually a nationwide professional league with the better existing American professional clubs as a nucleus.

Although the new conference survived only one season, it helped to pave the way for the impending professional soccer explosion of 1966. It was one of the preliminary steps on the long road towards acceptance of soccer as a major American professional sport.

The granting of territorial professional rights to the new United Soccer Association in late 1966 brought to an end the exclusive interstate professional jurisdiction in the East that had been granted by the United States Soccer Football Association to the American Soccer League in 1933. This decision brought about a change in the perspective of the American Soccer League as it sought to expand its area of activity into Washington, D.C., Rochester, New York, and Lowell, Massachusetts. The 1970 and 1971 seasons brought the league to a low ebb as only five teams competed in the schedule during these years. During 1969 the league had changed over to a summer season beginning in April and carrying on through August. However 1972 emerged as a year during which significant changes were to be made in the format of the organization. For the first time the American Soccer League was no longer an amalgamation primarily of ethnic oriented clubs, but a group that had become national in scope with three conferences in the Midwest, Northeast and Middle Atlantic sectors.

The 1973 season brought to a head a transition period during which the American Soccer League expanded into the Midwest and changed from a club conscious type of organization into a business-related sports enterprise.

In a 1974 effort to attract more attention from the national sports media and to open new avenues to investors, the league hired Bob Cousy, a former basketball "great" of Holy Cross and the Boston Celtics to become its Commissioner. It was reminiscent of the year 1926, when the "original" American Soccer League appointed Bill Cunningham, national syndicated sports writer and former All-American football player at Dartmouth College, to the post of Commissioner of its organization.

The appearance of Cousy, despite some skepticism, did bring about a program of expansion to the West Coast in 1976, converting for the first time the American Soccer League from an Eastern entity into a nationwide unit in professional soccer. By this time the league had become a full-fledged business venture.

Still, some sixty years after its inception, the American Soccer League mirrored the problems that have always beset the league. Ownerships and franchises have constantly been in flux, teams have been known to disintegrate in mid-season, inconsistent and inept organization and officiating has created instability, and promotional activities have fallen short of their goals. Only the ASL's most enthusiastic supporters would deny that the league operates in the shadow of the North American Soccer League.

The hope is that a league which encourages local American talent will attract the fan, with the outside support from television and other businesses.

Twice-daily calisthenics broke up the monotony for America's soccer stars during the long voyages to Europe and South America. Personal hardships were experienced by many players who had to leave their jobs for long periods.

11

EXPANDING
OUR HORIZONS
Relations with FIFA

OFFICIALS INDUSTRIAL LEAGUE. 1916

Soccer's organizers have always been the backbone of the sport. Here are the referee organizers for the Philadelphia Industrial League in 1916.

11

As an affiliate of the Federation Internationale de Football, Association (FIFA), the United States Football Association was able to participate in a world soccer competition for the first time at Paris in the Olympic Games of 1924. Thus the path had been opened for future American efforts in Olympic, Pan-American and World Cup tournaments.

Relations between F.I.F.A., the world body, and the United States Soccer Federation have not always been smooth. In 1928 the United States Football Association was embroiled in a controversy with FIFA relative to player-poaching tactics of the American professional clubs of the era. FIFA threatened the United States Football Assocation with suspension, but the problem was openly discussed and solved.

Almost forty years later, in 1967, the United States Soccer Football Association and FIFA were faced with a similar crisis, when "professional rights" and "organized soccer" were at stake. An ultimatum issued by FIFA to the United States Soccer Federation brought about an abrupt ending to the dissension.

Although most American professional sports shun foreign entanglements, FIFA membership through a national association offers certain benefits. The most obvious is the right of American teams to compete with and against teams of other nations in FIFA-sponsored events. It also gives worldwide validity to player contracts in a manner that precludes chaos in international relationships. At the amateur club level, membership offers very little advantage to the average player, official, college or high school team.

In the United States professional sports promotion is considered a business. In this respect it is subject to many government rules and regulations that are not always compatible with FIFA. FIFA has always insisted that a national body must control all phases of soccer in a particular country. In recent years the United States Soccer Federation constitution has omitted the term "control" and replaced it with the word "promote" in order to meet the legal exigency of the time and to avoid anti-trust litigation. It is unrealistic to expect that in a country as large as the United States, one agency could maintain air-tight control over all phases of a given sport.

Major professional league soccer at the present time is FIFA- and USSF-oriented and will likely remain so. Amateur club and semi-professional soccer, under the jurisdiction of the national body, has a strong ethnic tinge and has been pushed into relative obscurity by the emphasis on the major professional league game and by the surge in recent times of native-born youth participation. Despite its low-pressure image, however, the amateur game remains the backbone of the United States Soccer Federation.

The booming youth soccer movement has reached such explosive and varied proportions that it is no longer the exclusive domain of the USSF. Most municipal recreation programs now offer soccer programs, which understandably are unaffiliated with any particular national setup. Within the scope of these locally sponsored soccer activities are often encompassed both youth and adult summer endeavors.

College and high school soccer activities have a loose liaison with the United States Soccer Federation, but the control rests with their own regulatory bodies. So, just as America has 50 states, it probably has an equal number of ways of organizing leagues and other activities for the world's leading sport. It is not expected that all of soccer in America will ever be under the direction of one Association or Federation.

12
REFEREES
Vital to the Game

*George Young of Philadelphia was around when referees first began
to whistle American soccer. Young was an inspiration to aspiring
referees.*

12

A whistle did not exactly herald the beginning of American soccer. For years, games were played informally at best, with innocent and passive bystanders collared at the last moment to run the "games." Organization at the turn of the century brought referees together, and a few people started caring for and about referees.

Neither the task nor the identity of the referee has been at the forefront of American soccer. Little attention was paid to the plight, interests, or development of the "man in the middle." A young official was a rarity, in a world where ex-players would often take up the whistle only after experiencing retirement and empty Sunday afternoons.

Through the years, the laws changed little, and so did the atmosphere surrounding the referee, to say nothing of the referee himself. In a letter to an English referee magazine, New York referee Elman Dixon wrote in 1920: "Free expression of disagreement is a revered way of life in the United States, and the idea of a referee's decision being final is laughable. The result is open contempt for officialdom, even among prep school players. Referees are harangued, threatened, chased, and sometimes beaten, and it is a marvel that violence is not more frequent. I have been showered with more debris than dollars. I have been promised countless punches in the nose, and dozens of beatings. Twice I was threatened with lynching, and once with death."

In 1924, following their Olympic victory, the Uruguayan National team posed a problem which might have been a typical situation facing America's courageous referees. Playing a group of All-Stars in Newark, New Jersey, the visitors, described by a soccer writer as "possessing beauty and strength, acceleration and determination, and a symphony of art and power," proved lacking in sportsmanship. When a penalty kick was awarded to the home side, the Uruguayan captain promised a riot if the kick was made. The newspaper account: "The Newark man missed a golden opportunity. He should have scored his kick and let them march.

With all due respect to our guests, if they cannot accept a penalty whether they think they deserve it or not and insist on picking up their marbles and going home, I think that the courageous thing to do is help them gather up their toys and speed them on their way. Instead, the Newark man deliberately kicked the ball wide and made a bum of the referee." Other accounts indicate that soccer referees, players, and sometimes fans lived in fear of the violence that sometimes erupted from unthinking individuals, violence that seldom entered the domain of other sports.

The vast majority of soccer games were played on open public fields, as they are today, with players and spectators delighting in full support of the team, even at the expense of the official. Referees, however, were not deterred, and found support in their own group. On June 6, 1915 the USSFA instructed the various Referee Associations to organize themselves into a national body, and a few years later the United States Soccer Referees Association was granted associate membership in the USSFA, with full voting rights. Referees guided their own ship until 1937, when internal referee problems, coupled with disagreements with USSF led to the dissolution of the organization. State Associations were instructed to take over referee duties, and referees were brought under the immediate control of USSF, as they are today. Since that day, the only national referee organization has been the National Intercollegiate Soccer Officials Association.

13

THE DEAN OF
AMERICAN REFEREES
Jimmy Walder

George Moorhouse (left) of the New York Americans and Alec McNab (right) of the St. Louis Brewers were well-known figures to soccer fans in America in the 1920's. Jimmy Walder, tossing the coin, was America's most notable referee.

13

The referee who saw firsthand the development of American soccer is James A. "Jimmy" Walder of Philadelphia, Pennsylvania. Walder began his illustrious career as a referee in much the same way that coaches became coaches and other referees became referees: there was simply no one else around to do the job. So, in September 1909 on a damp Saturday afternoon at the Lighthouse Boys' Club field in Philadelphia, Jimmy "filled in" at a boys' game. Since that day his life was never the same; in fact he found time for little other than soccer.

Walder's career extended through seven decades, and he last appeared as a referee at the age of 84 at Christopher Lock High School in Lansdale, Pennsylvania in 1969. He whistled his first college game in 1913, continuing his activity in college officiating until 1965. The first official to wear the striped shirt, Walder's influence touched more than 50,000 players as he ran 34,000 miles on the field in his 4500 games. For 40 years he was chairman of the referee examining board for his referee association in Eastern Pennsylvania, and he counseled thousands of referees and coaches on the game.

While the statistical record of Walder's career is impressive and probably never to be broken, the man as a symbol of outstanding refereeing emerges over other achievements. He would "referee and bring himself to the level of the players," according to Eric Sellin, a fellow referee, never having complaints about the heat and emotion that would occasionally bring verbal and physical abuse. A large percentage of players he officiated spoke little English, and would do everything to take advantage of a frailty in an opponent or a referee. These people were encouraged by semi-hostile crowds and by many other referees who would call games to suit the home side. Once, in Newark, New Jersey, Walder found himself in the middle of a game that had to be abandoned. With both teams and supporters invading the field, and even the police fleeing the antagonized crowd, the diminutive Walder reluctantly left the field. Later he found himself in a hospital with knife wounds. Having returned to officiating less than a month later in the same stadium, he claimed at the time that getting attacked was "part of the game." Once even threatened with a gun by a hired "supporter," Walder was never known to hesitate on a penalty kick or player sanction because of the home crowd, and this honesty was not appreciated by all.

The Walder saga knew no bounds within the game. In 1913 he travelled to St. Louis and so impressed the soccer people there that he was offered a job and $25.00 a week to officiate in their leagues. In 1928, when six American Soccer League teams withdrew from the USSFA, Walder followed, and was fined $1000.00 by those very individuals who had counted on him to conduct so many of their important Cup games. A USSFA National Commission was set up to meet with him, and the fine was reduced to $30.00, with Walder reinstated. Because he was a leader of referees both on and off the field, he also became the center of controversy in 1938, when soccer referees throughout America went on a strike for four months. Again ensnarled with the governing body of soccer, Walder felt that full recognition should have been granted to the National Soccer Referees' Association, of which he was a central figure. An interesting sidelight of this strike is that referees, who were recruited "off the lots," were fully supported by the players. These formerly surly players were told to "accept all referees' decisions, regardless of personal views." Soccer, it had turned out, was peaceful, but without the emotion that accompanies hard physical play.

European soccer people saw Walder on seven different trips, where he represented the State Department in establishing overseas programs for American servicemen. In 1954, when almost 70, he stayed sixteen weeks for games, clinics, and appearances, continually selling the American game to both Americans and Europeans.

Countless referees who have never heard the name Walder are indebted to his missionary work for the game and for referees. With his friend Harry Rodgers, with whom he officiated 500 games, Walder invented the Two Referee System of Control, still in use in colleges, high schools, and in some youth soccer competitions. He proved a friend to all who touched a ball, and to those countless thousands who sat in the stands, helping to create an atmosphere of fairness and understanding.

14
COACHES
Known and Unknown

Bill Jeffrey, one of America's most noted coaches, lectures here for the Armed Forces in Europe following the close of World War II.

14

Prior to the organization of the National Soccer Coaches Association in 1941, the role of coach was often obscured on professional teams by the importance of the manager. The college and high school coach was visible but little appreciated, although he played an important role in the progress of the American college game prior to World War II.

One of the finest American coaches was Jim MacDonald, a Scotsman who managed the multi-starred Boston Wonder-Workers of the American Soccer League in the nineteen-twenties. Later he coached at Northeastern University in Boston, Harvard University and Brandeis University. MacDonald was far ahead of his time in his theories and he was instilling the very same soccer fundamentals into his charges that forty years later Detmar Cramer of Germany was extolling to new generations. Erno Schwartz, former Vienna Hakoah great and former American Soccer League business manager, was another highly rated coach, also producing the first coaching brochure for the United States Soccer Federation in 1948.

Douglas Stewart of the University of Pennsylvania was another old-time coach who had an influence on the development of American soccer tactics. As editor of the Intercollegiate Soccer Guide for many years, he wrote many articles on coaching. when such material was at a premium. During his coaching career at the University of Pennsylvania, his teams were soccer powers in the college ranks.

Bill Jeffrey shortly after World War II had a remarkable record as coach at Pennsylvania State College but the victory of the United States team, which he coached, over England in the World Cup of 1950 propelled him into international repute as a leader and soccer thinker.

There have been many excellent American coaches in both the professional and college ranks during the past two decades but time alone can properly evaluate them. Al Miller, former coach at Hartwick College, and Terry Fisher, another successful college coach and a player for Miller at Hartwick made their mark in both major professional soccer and the college game. Cliff McGrath, who played at Wheaton, has an excellent record at Seattle Pacific University. Bob Guelker at Southern Illinois University in Edwardsville established a fine coaching record at St. Louis University before shifting to Southern Illinois where he has continued to turn out strong teams. Harry Keough, coach at St. Louis University, has kept the St. Louis team in the upper echelon of college soccer. Both of these coaches have been able to compete effectively with American-born squads against those colleges that have depended upon recruiting foreign players.

In the not too distant future most American professional teams will be staffed by coaches of native American birth or coaches from overseas who have served an American apprenticeship and have acquired American citizenship.

Charles Scott, head coach at the University of Pennsylvania. Through the years, college coaches have closely cooperated with one another to improve the game.

15
GIANTS
AMONG THE PLAYERS

*Some members of the 1934 World Cup team pose as they make the transatlantic crossing to Rome.
Billy Gonsalves (third from left) is thought by many to be the greatest American player in the
game's history. (Photo, Courtesy of Walter Dick, player fourth from right.)*

15

Many great players have come and gone through American soccer history. Some have been native-born devotees of the game. Others have been Americans of foreign birth who have come from abroad as children with their parents. Many have been adult immigrants to the United States who have become American citizens. A few arrived as paid mercenaries to help bolster the strength of the wealthier clubs.

Tommy Swords of Fall River was the first native-born player to achieve national recognition in the 1905 to 1920 era. Harry Ratican of St. Louis and Bethlehem Steel was another native American player who attained prominence, also during the same era.

The defection from British soccer of Tommy Muirhead, Jock McIntyre and Alec McNabb, Scottish Internationalists and Mickey Hamil, an Irish Internationalist, to Boston of the American Soccer League in 1924 created as much of a stir in that day as did the coming of Pele into the North American Soccer League in 1975. Other native sons were Billy Gonsalves of Fall River and Boston, Davie Brown of Newark, Pete Renzulli of New York, Tommy Florie of New Jersey, Millard Lang of Baltimore, Pete Donelli of Pittsburgh, Bert Patenaude of Fall River and Arnie Oliver of New Bedford. Archie Stark, although born in Scotland, came to America in his early teens and developed into one of America's finest players.

In the post-World War II period John Souza of Fall River was the outstanding homebred player, always impressing British and European experts with his talent. Ed Souza, another Fall River player, Harry Keough and Charles Colombo of St. Louis, and Walter Bahr of Philadelphia are other native born players who excelled in international soccer in the same time period.

During the past two decades many more American bred players have made their debuts in worldwide soccer. As the future of American soccer unfolds, some of them will earn places alongside the elite of American tradition.

Kyle Rote, Jr. is America's first modern superstar. Though he did not play soccer until after high school, his physique, attitude, and intelligence enabled him to excel in the North American Soccer League.

16
SOME GREAT
AMERICAN GAMES

The first great national final in USFA history was played in 1915 in Bethlehem, Pennsylvania, when the Bethlehem Football Club played the Brooklyn Celtic Football Club. The game was the first $1000.00 gate in the sport in America.

16

There have been many memorable games during the long history of American soccer.

Before 8,000 enthusiastic supporters, Fall River defeated the Corinthians of England by 3 goals to 0 at Fall River, Massachusetts in 1906. The Corinthians had won nine straight games by top heavy scores during its United States tour and the result helped to restore faith in America and its soccer progress. The Corinthians were a strong combination of English League players.

Another epoch in the annals of American soccer was the victory of the Fall River Rovers, with a lineup that included nine native-born players, over the Bethlehem Steel eleven with its professional imports from abroad in the National Open Cup Final of 1917. It was a game that brought homebred players to the forefront in United States competition.

Three years later the native-born Ben Millers of St. Louis brought homebred soccer to its zenith with a 2-1 win at St. Louis in the National Open Cup Final in 1920 against Fore River of Quincy, Massachusetts. The Fore River team fielded a preponderance of old country professional talent.

In 1924 the United States participated in the Olympic Games for the first time. The American team defeated Estonia in the initial round but succumbed to the eventual champions Uruguay in the second round by a 3-0 tally. It established the creditability of American soccer on the international plane.

American soccer prestige was given a boost at the first World Cup Games in Uruguay in 1930. The United States finished in third place. Despite attempts in some quarters to depreciate the achievement, the American team performed well. It was a truly American team with both native-born and foreign-born American citizens on exhibit. In the semifinals the United States team was defeated by Argentina 6-1, after holding the South American team to a one goal deficit in the first half. It is seldom mentioned that the American eleven was playing well until one of the players was injured a short time into the second half. The team finished with ten men.

Another notable performance by an American team, even in defeat, occurred at the Olympic Games in Berlin, Germany during 1936. The United States eleven battled the Italian team in a game that ended with a 1-0 win for the European representative. Italy wound up as the champion of the tournament.

The outstanding achievement by a representative American soccer eleven was accomplished at the 1950 World Cup Games in Brazil when the United States team, with eight native-born players, won over England 1-0. It was the greatest upset in World Cup history. Although the event passed almost unnoticed by the news media in the United States, some observers felt it would herald the beginning of the United States' climb as a world soccer power.

The advent of the United Soccer Association as a new American professional venture in 1967 produced one of the most dramatic games ever played in the United States. In the championship play-off on July 14 the Los Angeles Wolves, playing at home, defeated the Washington Whips 6 to 5 in sudden-death overtime after 126 minutes of play.

The turning point in American professional soccer came on August 14, 1977 at Giants Stadium in the Meadowlands of New Jersey when a crowd of 77,691 filled every seat to watch the New York Cosmos vanquish the Ft. Lauderdale Strikers 8 goals to 3. It was the largest attendance at a soccer game in more than 100 years of American soccer history.

Less than 60 days later, a game in the same stadium marked the final international tribute to Pele, the greatest player in the history of the game. Honoring his retirement as a player, 72,000 attended a game on October 1, 1977 between the only two teams he had been associated with as a player, Santos of Brazil and the Cosmos. Played in the pouring rain, the game ended in a 2-1 victory for the American club. Pele played half the game for each team, scoring a first-half goal for the Cosmos. Known as Pele to the world, Edson to his friends, and Dico to his family, this one man had brought to light what lesser men had not accomplished in decades of hard work: acceptance of the game among Americans. His final exit exhibited the emotion of the game, the crowd, and of those who play it.

There are those who feel that the greatest American game will be a triumph at the World Cup level, or at the Final itself. Others are content with less, recognizing that neither the size of the crowd nor the prestige of the game is what makes a game "great." For them it may be a game that is even, well-played, and in the best spirit of sport.

17

THE 1950 WORLD CUP
America Shocks
All But America

Moments before the end, England attacks the American goal at Belo Horizonte. Roy Bentley (dark shirt) of England and Harry Keough go up for the ball, but Frank Borghi will easily save. At game's end, the 40,000 spectators stormed the field and helped the Americans celebrate. Less than 50 Americans saw this greatest upset in World Cup history.

17

Even in 1950, soccer could not seriously be considered a popular sporting pursuit of many Americans. When the United States team traveled to Belo Horizonte, Brazil for the World Cup, few noticed. A few days later, when the shocking 1-0 American victory over England was announced, it was dutifully and routinely reported in the American press. To the American soccer enthusiast, however, it represented great hope for the future, and called attention to America's progress.

The Associated Press dispatch of June 29th, 1950 was clear and concise. It read:

> "The United States today defeated England 1-0 to add the latest and biggest upset in the world soccer championships. The favored British team and the spectators were stunned by the result. The lone tally of the match was scored by Joe Gaetjens at 39 minutes of the first half.
>
> "Brazilian fans swarmed onto the field after the United States victory and took the Americans on their shoulders while the victors were given an ovation. The British forwards were uncertain in aiming for goal but their general play appeared superior to that of the winners except on the scoreboard. The United States, under pressure, gave up six corner kicks to England's two."

It was an upset of the first magnitude to those followers of soccer beyond the confines of the United States who had been loathe to accept the emergence of the American game. Destiny beckoned the American team, when in a game with the touring All-England team prior to their departure for Brazil, the United States squad held England to a 1-0 score at Randalls Island, New York. It was a harbinger of things to come.

Various reasons were given for the defeat of England. John Graydon in the *English Saturday Post* stated, "Williams in the England goal positioned himself perfectly to gather in Bahr's shot but Gaetjens, the American leader, ruined everything for him. Gaetjens jumped in, failed to connect with his forehead but the ball accidentally hit the top of his head —

and was deflected into the England goal." At half time America still held the lead but English Manager Walter Winterbottom had no criticism to make of his team: "Go on playing good football and the goals will come," he told his team.

The refereeing was subjected to considerable criticism by some. An inference was made that an American defender had saved a goal by kicking the ball back into play after it had entered the goal and passed over the goal-line. It was also alleged that an American defender threw himself through the air in the penalty area to grab Mortensen of England who had only the goalkeeper to beat. The Italian referee awarded a freekick outside of the penalty-area.

The claim that Gaetjens misjudged the ball and accidently deflected it into the goal was a premise of so-called soccer experts who were hesitant to acknowledge the quality of American soccer. Gaetjens during the 1949-1950 season was the leading scorer with 18 goals in the rugged American Soccer League. His goal at Belo Horizonte was from a diving header. Eight of the players on the American team were native born and all were fine soccer performers of world standard. McIlvenny, a Scotsman, Maca, a Belgian and Gaetjens, a Haitian, were the only members of the eleven who were foreign born.

The only cloud over the proceedings was the fact these foreign born players technically were not American citizens, although resident Americans. All three of the players returned to their homelands shortly afterwards.

Walter Bahr of the United States team summed it up best when he said: "Everyone knows the better team does not always win. How many times has a third or fourth division team beaten a second or first division team in Cup play? All sports are filled with upsets. That is what sport is all about."

Perhaps the United States victory at Belo Horizonte was not a surprise after all, but a refusal by overseas soccer disciples to acknowledge the latent American soccer potential.

Seventeen players composed the United States roster for the World Competition in 1950. Frank Borghi, Harry Keough, Charles Colombo, Frank Wallace, and Cino Pariani of St. Louis, Joseph Maca and Edward McIlvenny of New York, Joseph Gaetjens of New York, Walter Bahr of Philadelphia and John and Edward Sousa of Fall River competed against England. The balance of the squad included Robert Annis of St. Louis, Jeffrey Coombes of Chicago, Robert Craddock and Nick Di Orio of Pittsburgh and Gino Gardassanich and Adam Wolanin of Chicago. Bill Jeffrey of Pennsylvania State College and Walter Giesler of St. Louis, the coach and manager, respectively, completed the entourage.

18
INTERNATIONAL TOURNAMENT
1960 — 1965

The influence of visiting foreign teams may have lined the pockets of promoters and aided the USSF, but many felt it had no effect on the development of the game in America. Here, America Soccer Club of Brazil meets Dukla of Czechoslovakia at Soldier's Field in Chicago, August 1962.

18

The National Commission of the United States Soccer Federation in July 1958 received a request from the American Soccer League through its business manager Erno Scwarcz, that was of great import to the future of professional soccer in America.

The American Soccer League presented a plan for the creation of an International Soccer League that would involve top caliber European teams and clubs from Canada and the United States. The matter was referred to the 1959 United States Soccer Federation Convention. At this meeting the American Soccer League received permission to go ahead with the project.

In 1960 under the sponsorship of the American Soccer League, the International Soccer Tournament became a reality with a competition of imported foreign teams. William Cox, the former owner of the Philadelphia Phillies of the National Baseball League, was well versed in the operation of a major professional sports enterprise. The only drawback to the plan was the fact that the success of the endeavor was predicated upon an appeal to the nationalistic instincts of the many ethnic groups of Greater New York City that would be represented by visiting teams from their homelands. In a larger sense the main premise for introducing this international type of competition was to provide a testing ground for determining if soccer had a "grass roots" appeal for the American sporting public. Indirectly, it was also intended to eventually pave the way for an attempt to establish soccer on a major nationwide professional footing.

The International Tournament during its first season in the summer of 1960 was centered in New York City but in subsequent years it also encompassed other cities. The opening game at the Polo Grounds in New York City drew 10,000 fans to watch Kilmarnock of Scotland and Bayern Munchen of Germany. In the final game of the season Bangu of Brazil, winner of the first section, defeated Kilmarnock, the titleholder in the second division, by a 2-0 score to become the first champion of the International Soccer League before 25,000 spectators.

From 1960 through 1965 these annual tournaments were ambitious experiments that fulfilled their early promise to prepare the groundwork for future professional league ventures. They produced world class soccer for American sports fans with a competitive tinge. The tournaments were conducted in a league context with a play-off between the division winners and a final challenge round with the current year's champion meeting the challenge round winner from the previous year. Many world renowned teams such as Werden Bremen and Bayern Munich of Germany, Hearts and Kimarnock of Scotland, Dukla of Czechoslovakia, AEK of Holland, Blackburn Rovers of England, Red Star from Yugoslavia and Bangu from Brazil among others participated at one time or another during the existence of the competition. In 1965 a New York team was entered in the tournament with a lineup recruited from the German American League plus three British imports. This club surprised the experts by winning the title in its division against strong European and South American opposition. In 1967, the tournament was terminated when the promoters and the America Soccer League parted ways.

19
WOMEN AND GIRLS IN AMERICAN SOCCER

Soccer has turned into a family game in America, as in no other country. Meet the Ed Fosmire family of La Mirada, California . . . . . all soccer players.

19

Oscar Wilde once said, "Soccer may be perfectly all right for tough girls, but not the right sport for gentle lads."

The current influence of women and girls on American soccer has been just one more commentary on the game's universal appeal. No one would argue that female fans, players, coaches, and referees in America are more active than anywhere in the world. In recent years more than one-third of spectators at professional games are women. While there are no female professional players, they compete at every other level, playing a skilled, exciting, and always competitive game.

The 1920s brought several incidents of women's entry into soccer, long before the general population knew much about the game, and at a time when in other sports women were relegated to the sidelines. In the Fall of 1927, Slacia Penata, a girl, played regular goalkeeper for the Central Falls, Rhode Island Senior Amateur club. It is highly possible that she was influenced by the United States appearance of Dick Kerr's Ladies Professional Soccer Team in 1922. These skilled English players won three games, tied three, and lost two against top men's amateur clubs on the Eastern Seaboard. They outscored the opposition, 35-34, and proved that the game could be played well by athletes of either sex.

Also in the 1920s Alfredda Inglehart, the only woman now in the Soccer Hall of Fame, began her 30 year teaching career in athletics, during which she taught more than 1200 boys in the fundamentals of the game. Many became top-flight professionals, including Bill Scwange, Bob Delashmutt, Johnny Skerry, Topsy Hartung, and Alec Sparra. Millard Lang, another "pupil," became a member in the U.S. Soccer Hall of Fame as well.

It was not until the early 1960s, however, that girls were seen playing soccer in any appreciable numbers, having left the traditional confines of speedball and field hockey. At first, mixed leagues were formed, but girls found themselves more interested in "separate but equal" leagues. High schools and colleges as well now have difficulty keeping up with the demands of girls wanting to continue in the sport. In 1978, the Ivy League crowned its first champion, Harvard University, and women's soccer proved it had arrived. At the same time, the Dallas Sting returned from an international competition in Taiwan, having placed third. This tournament was hailed as a success for women's soccer and for the United States' involvement in the world game.

The enthusiasm (and sometimes the skills) of girls is no less than that of the boys.

20
CLOSE TO THE
WORLD'S BEST
The American Girl Player

Diana Bohn of the "Sting," with her cup awarded to the 25 top players in the 1978 World Women's Football Tournament. Diana scored 6 of her team's 8 goals in their games.

20

The progress of American soccer as manifested in women's play first made itself known in October 1978. The "Sting," a well-organized and highly competitive team of 16-20 year olds, was invited to the World's Women's Football Tournament. Playing in Taipei, Taiwan before as many as 30,000 spectators each game, the Dallas, Texas girls placed a very respectable third in the tournament. The competition brought some national teams, semi-professional sides, and All-Star clubs from Canada, England, France, Finland, Sweden, Polynesia, Austria, Australia, The Republic of China, Switzerland, Thailand, and Denmark.

The level of play in each case represented the best of the countries. American soccer, it was felt, was very competitive with the world's best. The STING's record during the eight day tournament:

STING (United States)			
1	Sweden	1
1	Australia	1
1	Austria	0
2	Republic of China	0
0	Finland	2
0	France	0
3	Switzerland	2

Loser of only one game on American soil, the STING has also traveled to Mexico, Sweden, and England. Under coaches Bill Kinder, Chet Mills, and John Fougeron, the club also fields a "B" team, with younger reserve players who later compete for the first squad.

The American method of attacking the ball at all times, coupled with close team spirit, has served the Sting well. Good competition in girl's and women's soccer is sparse, and the Sting has to look far and wide for adequate competition. As Diana Bohn, now graduated from the "Under 19" program, points to another problem, that of adequate programs for mature and spirited players: "There's no where to go. Competitive girls in America shouldn't have to retire at age 20."

Everyone has fun at a high school soccer game in Centerville, Ohio, and that's why games are consistently sold out. Soccess in high school soccer is the result of enthusiasm and hard work.

21
THE HIGH SCHOOL GAME

The high school game in the 1940s and 1950s was largely confined to the Northeast. Note the lack of nets, now a rarity.

21

Soccer of sorts has been played formally or informally in the schools of the United States since the 1860s. Only since the turn of the century, however, has the game actually made consistent inroads into the athletic programs of the public schools.

New York City was the first municipality to include soccer as a part of the athletic curriculum, doing so in the Fall of 1905. The school authorities in such cities as Boston, Philadelphia, Baltimore, Newark, and other cities in the East by 1920 had introduced soccer into their elementary schools and in some cases had extended the game into their high school activities. In the Midwest, St. Louis, and in the Far West San Francisco, Los Angeles and Salt Lake City had fostered the sport in some of their elementary grades on an intra-mural basis.

For many years high schools, influenced by the professional and college football element, were reluctant to accept soccer as a varsity sport but in the elementary schools it was viewed as an acceptable physical activity. In New York, Pennsylvania, New Jersey, Maryland, Delaware, Massachusetts, Connecticut, Rhode Island and New Hampshire, some private preparatory and public high schools were participating in soccer in the era before World War I.

During the 1920s and 1930s, high school soccer began to receive grudging acceptance from enlightened school administrators, continuing to have its main roots in the East. An occasional team or league was found in the Midwest or on the Pacific Coast.

Beginning in 1946 secondary school soccer began its unprecedented growth which by the 1960s and 1970s had approached explosive proportions. The National Federation of High School Athletic Associations no longer looked upon soccer as a stepchild, giving it full recognition.

In 1971 a total of 1768 high schools in 24 states had placed soccer on their athletic programs, and two years later the number had exceeded 2300 schools in 39 states. By 1977 the statistics found soccer as a major sport in more than 4000 high schools, as 160,000 players competed. This total included 18,000 girls.

Youth soccer as a Saturday community activity has been a great factor in the advancement of soccer in these school areas that had neglected the game over the years. Pressures developed by the youth movement within the school systems eliminated much of the hypocrisy that had previously suppressed the sport.

The training and development of young soccer players in early programs has helped high school soccer.

22
OTTO HAAS AND
CHATHAM, NEW JERSEY

Otto Haas' understanding of young players is his most important quality. Here he welcomes two of his former players who have returned to see Chatham record another victory.

22

When Otto Haas took over the soccer program at Chatham, New Jersey High School in 1947, no one could possibly have expected what would follow. With him he brought only high school playing experience, for college soccer was just starting at his alma mater, Colgate University.

More than 30 years and 500 games later, Haas represents quality coaching in a sport that has seen many changes. In 1947, Chatham was the only team in Morris County. Now, where the offspring of Haas' earliest players are competing, there are 28 schools, as well as numerous girls' programs. Coaching is much better, youth programs provide an endless array of talent, and the game is no longer seasonal. Most of Chatham's rivals shoot for their big game against the "Eskimos," and some of them even prepare in winter months.

Through it all, the Chatham program remains an outstanding example of consistent, positive, and informed leadership. Team practices indicate unusual motivation among players, and the steady, guiding hand of Haas is visible in every drill and exercise. Players also know there is no place for any sort of ungentlemanly conduct in the program. In these 30 years, only one Chatham player has been sent off a field by a referee! Haas, who officiated many years in colleges, never complains about referees, and referees are not discussed during those rare Chatham losses.

The supply of talent is endless in Chatham, and varsity games frequently see the first team on the bench after halftime as substitutes gain valuable game experience. Hundreds of Chatham players have gone on to college. John Rennie, coach of Duke University is a Chatham graduate, as well as several high school coaches.

Otto Haas' secrets are hidden in modesty and in a community which expects success. "Our players always think they are a bit better than they are, and I guess it helps them play better," says the Verona, New Jersey High School graduate, who once played soccer against Chatham, and whose son James was once selected as the top soccer player in New Jersey.

Otto Haas' Coaching Record

Won   403   Lost   68   Tied   58

Six undefeated seasons

Longest Winning Streak: 52 games

16 State Championships (Runners-Up, Four times)

Three Times New Jersey Soccer Coach of the Year

Goals For: 1563   Against: 418

Never had a losing season

Otto Haas displays the steel-toed shoe which players wore when he began coaching. Each shoe also had more than 200 nails in the sole. No wonder shin-guards were so popular.

23
THE COLLEGE GAME

The college game was struggling just following World War II. Here, Boston University in white is pitted against Tufts University (dark shirts). Many college players competed semi-professionally on the weekends.

23

American college before the 1860s was a nondescript form of the game with playing rules that varied from college to college. On November 6, 1869 Princeton and Rutgers met at New Brunswick, New Jersey under Rutgers' rules in a game that initiated intercollegiate soccer in the United States. These rules were a reasonable fascimile of the Football Association of England code. Rutgers won the game, 6-4. Soccer was the Fall sport of the colleges until 1876, when the Intercollegiate Football Association was organized at Springfield, Massachusetts. The rules of English rugby displaced the soccer laws to govern competition. It heralded the eclipse of soccer as an intercollegiate sport for three decades until 1905.

A furore was created in football circles when President Theodore Roosevelt threatened to eliminate the sport as a college pastime in 1905 unless the violence and mayhem were controlled. It renewed hopes among soccer followers that the college authorities would see the light and elevate their game to a place of prominence on the college campuses. Although the hope never materialized, it did muster sufficient support for the formation of an Intercollegiate Soccer League for the 1906 season, with Columbia, Cornell, Harvard, Haverford and Pennsylvania competing.

Until 1914 the league played its games in the Spring, as organizers felt unwilling to compete directly with football and baseball. Later, it was decided to change the season to the Fall months. The year 1914 also brought soccer innovation, with the approval of a substitution rule for injured players. The rule was resisted by FIFA for almost 50 years.

Although the league was reorganized after the end of hostilities in 1919 it soon became apparent that the growth of soccer in the colleges necessitated a larger association to accommodate the new college teams. In 1925 the original Intercollegiate Soccer League was disbanded and its members became the nucleus of the new Intercollegiate Soccer Association. During the depression years of the 1930s regional leagues were developed in the Middle Atlantic states and in New England.

The modern era, beginning in 1946, has seen a tremendous expansion in the college game. By the end of 1946 there were 86 colleges playing the sport in the United States. From 1946 until 1978 the number of colleges that had become part of the soccer picture had increased to almost 1000.

The formation of the National Soccer Coaches Association in 1941 had been a landmark event in the progress of American intercollegiate soccer. It had provided a forum for ideas for the coaches from all regions of the United States and it created a working organization for a concerted effort. Many innovations were sponsored for college soccer by the coaches group.

On December 14, 1946 the first All-Star Intercollegiate game was played at Sterling Oval, New York city, when an All-South team with players from the Mid-Atlantic states and the Southern states defeated a North team with New York and New England players, 1-0. During 1947-1948 college players were seriously considered for the United States Olympic squad, another indication of college soccer's arrival.

At Sportsmen's Park in St. Louis on New Year's Day 1950 more than 5,000 spectators watched Penn State and San Francisco tie, 1-1, inaugurating the first Soccer Bowl game.

In December 1956 the forerunner of the National Championships was staged when West Chester (Pennsylvania) State College defeated Springfield College 1-0 in the Eastern Intercollegiate play-offs. The National Intercollegiate Soccer Championships were held for the first time at Storrs, Connecticut where St. Louis won the final game 5 to 2 over Bridgeport in 1959. The annual Senior Soccer Bowl came into existence at Winter Park, Florida when the East won over the West by a 2-0 score.

One of the encouraging features of American Intercollegiate soccer has been the success of colleges that have drawn upon American-born talent for their players in competition with schools that have depended upon foreign imports for their players. Indeed, the game had progressed far beyond the time when Tom Cahill, National Secretary of U.S.S.F.A. derisively referred to the college player as a "jumping jack."

24

HARRY KEOUGH AND
SAINT LOUIS UNIVERSITY

Coach Harry Keough of St. Louis University (left) has never had to go far to recruit players. Even closer to home was son Ty (right), a 1978 All-American.

24

The oldest university west of the Mississippi River, though located in the middle of a soccer-conscious community, didn't officially recognize the game until 1959. Initiated by Bob Guelker, the success of the program was immediate.

Today, Harry Keough carries on the tradition, and few would argue that the St. Louis University Billikens' soccer means quality. Though St. Louis high school graduates are found on campuses all over America, there has always been talent enough for all, and Keough continues developing players into championship teams. Aided by Assistant Coaches Miguel de Lima and Val Pelizzaro, Keough can watch his players grow through the junior leagues of the city. He has never had to recruit outside of his own environment, even though he had no home field at the university and can offer only eleven scholarships.

Tradition at St. Louis includes an unrelenting schedule with few "easy wins," all pointing to preparation for the national play-offs. A physical regimen which discourages some, and a game of soccer which centers on teamwork and on limited individual ball control, points to a hard and fast game. Keough, who points out that America's first soccer scholarship went to a St. Louis boy (Ronald Coleman, 1948, Pennsylvania State University), totally endorses the St. Louis Catholic Youth Council Program. Players there start at age 5 or 6. Keough, a supervisor with the U.S. Postal Service, dreams of the time when the college game will be on campus, enjoyed by more than the average 2000 people who now see the Billikens.

St. Louis University

Bob Guelker's record (1959 through 1966, eight years):

Games Played	Won	Lost	Tied	Goals For	Goals Against
109	95	10	4	572	95

Harry Keough's record (1967 through 1978, 12 years):

211	166	30	15	585	182

Totals	320	261	40	19	1157	277

Ten NCAA Championships:
1959, 60, 62, 63, 65
1967, 69, 70, 72, 73

25
PROFESSIONAL SOCCER
IS HERE . . . . 1967 — 1979

Professional soccer's first sellout crowds were in San Jose, California in 1974 where the Earthquakes combined attacking soccer with solid front-office promotion.

25

The rebirth of American professional major league soccer in 1967 was spurred on by a national viewing of the 1966 World Cup Final from England. It started auspiciously with the United Soccer Association, recognized by the United States Soccer Federation. The National Professional Soccer League, an independent group, was also searching for approval from the American sports public.

The United Soccer Association did not intend to begin operations until 1968, but was caught off guard by the plans of the National Professional Soccer League to play in 1967. To meet the exigencies of the situation it was decided to import entire teams from abroad on a lend-lease arrangement, to represent the twelve franchises for the summer season of 1967.

The summer playing season in the United States coincides with the European off season, making this emergency program feasible. The National Professional Soccer League placed ten teams on the field and stocked their rosters with American and foreign talent acquired under direct individual contracts.

The rosters of clubs for both leagues shaped up as follows for the 1967 season:

UNITED SOCCER ASSOCIATION: Boston (Shamrock Rovers, Ireland), Cleveland (Stoke City, England), Detroit (Glentoran, Ireland), New York (Cerro, Uruguay), Toronto (Hibernian, Scotland), Dallas (Dundee United, Scotland), Houston (Bangu, Brazil), Los Angeles (Wolverhampton, England), San Francisco (Ado Den Haag, Holland), Vancouver (Sunderland, England), Chicago (Cagliari, Italy), Washington (Aberdeen, Scotland).

NATIONAL PROFESSIONAL SOCCER LEAGUE: Atlanta, Baltimore, Chicago, Los Angeles, New York, Philadelphia, Pittsburgh, Oakland, St. Louis, Toronto.

The 1967 professional season made an impact on the American public nationwide but the strife incurred between the United Soccer Association and the National Professional Soccer League contending for supremacy, boded ill for the future. In the United Soccer Association final the Los Angeles team defeated Washington 6 to 5 in overtime for the championship, in what may have been the most exciting professional game in American history. In the National Professional League Oakland beat Baltimore 4 to 2 in a two game, total goals series for the league top honors. Oakland is still thought to be the greatest professional team ever assembled in America.

By 1968 the two leagues, under the pressure of anti-trust allegations in the background, worked out a merger plan. From it all emerged the North American Soccer League. It was in the nature of a "Shot-gun" wedding, urged on by FIFA.

Seventeen clubs were ready for the beginning of the 1968 season. Without a television contract, the expected revenues failed to materialize. Many of the high powered executives who had vowed to stay with professional soccer for ten years lost their effervesence when faced with mounting financial deficits. The Atlanta Chiefs of the former National Professional Soccer League won the league title with a 3 to 0 victory over the San Diego Toros in the play-offs, as the NASL struggled on.

The 1969 season was almost a disaster after twelve clubs faded from the league. Five franchises surviving were Atlanta, Baltimore, Dallas, Kansas City and St. Louis, all supported by men with some vision and money. Kansas City won the championship.

During 1970 six clubs were available for the beginning of the summer season. Baltimore had withdrawn from the league but the Washington Darts and Rochester Lancers of the American League had crossed over to the rival North American Soccer League. In the two game play-offs Rochester was victorious over Washington by the aggregate score of 4 to 3, an event of significant import to the proponents of the American Soccer League.

The North American Soccer League by 1971 had retrenched itself sufficiently to place eight franchises in two divisions at Montreal, New York, Toronto, Dallas, Atlanta, Rochester, St. Louis and Washington. Kansas City had withdrawn with the return of baseball to that city. The Dallas Tornado won the championship with a two out of three games victory over the Atlanta Chiefs.

The League maintained its status quo with eight teams again in 1972 as the New York Cosmos defeated the St. Louis Stars in the final play-off.

By 1973 the North American Soccer League had increased to nine clubs, as a new team, the Philadelphia Atoms won over the Dallas Tornado

2 to 0 in the play-off. Coach Al Miller of the Philadelphia Atoms became the first native American coach to lead a team to the North American Professional League title.

It was in 1974 that the league expanded to fifteen clubs and once again became a continent-wide organization with teams in San Jose, Los Angeles, San Francisco and Vancouver. Boston, Baltimore and Denver also joined the league Atlanta and Montreal disbanded. Los Angeles defeated the Miami Toros 4 to 3 in a tie-breaker for the league championship before a nationwide television audience. The San Jose Earthquakes, with sellout crowds of 19,000 proved for the first time in American soccer history that the non-soccer public could be won over the the game.

By 1975 twenty teams had acquired franchises. Chicago, Hartford, Portland, San Antonio and Tampa Bay had been added to the league. The Tampa Bay Rowdies, a new team, gained a 2 to 0 victory over the Portland Timbers, another freshman club, in the play-offs for the title. Both Tampa and Minnesota had played before large and enthusiastic home crowds, thus increasing the number of cities in which "Americanization" had taken place.

The 1976 season saw further changes in the North Americn Soccer League roster. Baltimore shifted to San Diego and Denver located in Minnesota. In the Soccer Bowl of 1976 Toronto won from Minnesota 3 to 0.

There were more changes in the roster of the North American Soccer League teams in 1977. Hartford was moved to New Haven, Miami wound up at Ft. Lauderdale. San Diego became Las Vegas and San Antonio jumped to Hawaii. Boston and Philadelphia faded from the scene. In the Soccer Bowl of 1977 the New York Cosmos with Pele in action defeated Seattle 2 goals to 1 at Portland, Oregon before a capacity crowd of 35,548. An American record soccer crowd of 77,691 watched the New York Cosmos win over Ft. Lauderdale 8 to 3 at Giants Stadium, East Rutherford, New Jersey in the second game of the play-off series.

The alignment of teams for the 1978 season found 24 teams ready for action. Six new teams were added to the league in the off season: Colorado Caribous, Tulsa Roughnecks, New England Teamen, Philadelphia Fury, Detroit Express, Memphis Rogues and Houston Hurricane were the newcomers. Four clubs had a change of venue. St. Louis moved to California, Hawaii transferred to Tulsa, Las Vegas located in San Diego and Connecticut found a new home in Oakland. The Cosmos defeated the Tampa Bay Rowdies for the championship, 3-0.

Since the formation of the United Soccer Association and the National Professional Soccer League in 1967 and the subsequent North American Soccer League, professional soccer has continued to depend largely upon temporary imports from Europe, Africa, Central America and South America for its basic talent. American players, largely from the colleges, have been signed to augment the squads but in many cases these players have been token members of the teams with infrequent appearances in the line-ups in order to maintain a "Made in America" image.

Most of the foreign players have been under contract to professional teams in their homelands. They have been acquired by the American clubs on lend-lease agreements for duty in the United States during the hiatus period between the playing seasons in other lands, which usually coincides with the professional league summer season in the United States. With the ever changing personnel it has been almost impossible for teams to maintain that continuity of playing talent from season to season that is so essential, if player charisma is to be built up and exploited at the box office.

Other American professional sports teams possess exclusive control over the contracts of their players. It is a more costly process but it does ensure relative club stability and proper recognition by the news media. Fortunately, the present policy of American professional clubs calls for gradual replacement of foreign mercenaries on loan.

Recently, more and more North American Soccer League and American Soccer League teams have been acquiring foreign players on exclusive contracts. This trend with the use of a greater proportion of American players of both foreign and native birth has made the direction of the league more apparent. The New York Cosmos are a prime example of this tendency with world class players such as Pele, Beckenbauer, Chinaglia, Bogicevic, and Marinho acquired on exclusive contracts.

The coming of age of professional soccer in the United States has caused consternation in Britain and Continental Europe and a decided blow to the patronizing and condescending acceptance that has always characterized the overseas attitude towards American soccer.

26
A CONTRIBUTOR
FROM BRAZIL

Pele chose America as the site for his final game. Overcome with emotion, he bade the game fare-well in Meadowlands Stadium, October 1977.

26

The coming of Pele to the United States lent credibility worldwide to the high standard of American professional soccer. It was the $4,500,000 contract which he received in 1975, however, that earned the recognition of the news media and the American sporting public as a whole. The European skeptics, who traditionally have consoled themselves by designating players who abandoned British, European and South American soccer to join the American professional ranks as "has-beens," were flabbergasted by the Pele move and the size of his contract terms. It was a body blow to those overseas experts who had depreciated American soccer for decades.

Pele's charisma and undeniable skills brought Americans of all persuasions to the 90 games he played with the Cosmos. Although he had already played in 65 countries and scored over 1100 goals in a career that began almost 20 years before the Cosmos, Pele had a special mission, and that was to bring the game to the people. Overflow crowds welcomed him wherever he went, in the only country in the world where he could still walk unrecognized on the busiest of streets. He conducted clinics and promotions, sat patiently, even enthusiastically through interviews, but found his greatest joy in working and relating to children. In the youth of America and of the world he viewed his own innocence and trust. More than one observer noted that he would never leave a location until the children had obtained their picture, and enjoyed personal contact with the man who radiated the simple pleasures of his game.

The "Pele Generation" proudly posed with the legend, then went out to imitate his skills.

27
THE PELE GENERATION
Born in the 1960's
Playing in the 1970's

The American Youth Soccer Organization, founded in 1964 in California, pointed the way for full participation for its thousands of players. Bench-sitting immediately became a thing of the past, as each player would play at least half of each game.

27

There are soccer observers who contended that the sport had interest for a very limited audience . . . an immigrant population reliving its past. While that statement has no credibility today, it could be said that soccer's appeal to America's youth did not really begin until the 1970s.

Certainly there were scattered programs, with tireless organizers, capable referees, and qualified coaches. However, these leagues were the exception, and were often "select" leagues for boys only. Almost overnight, with the coming of the 1970s, came the youngsters' realization that soccer offered something "different."

The game reached all of America, through clubs, church and recreational leagues, and the schools. YMCA leagues, with large programs in cities such as Dallas and Atlanta, brought the game to youngsters in large metropolitan areas. The United States Soccer Federation, with its United States Youth Soccer Association, has registered players in most states, and currently is directed by Tom Fleck in Pennsylvania. The American Youth Soccer Organization, under the able direction of one of its founders, Hans Stierle, currently lists almost 200,000 participants in twenty-five states.

With 5,000,000 boys and girls now developing their skills, the optimists now predict 20,000,000 players in America by 1990. The youth are probably the key to the direction of soccer in the future, for they will want to continue playing as young and middle-aged adults. Unlike their own parents, they will teach their own youngsters the joys of kicking, heading, and passing a ball.

In October 1977, on the day of Pele's retirement, hundreds of young players ringed the field at Meadowlands in New Jersey in tribute to their hero, the man who brought soccer to America on a large-scale basis. The announcer proclaimed the young players as the "Pele Generation." As this generation emerges and grows, along with it will follow those who have been waiting and watching.

The organizational problems were temporarily forgotten when the "big game" was played. The winners stand, and the losers are seated here at a junior championship in 1928.

28
THE UNITED STATES
SOCCER FEDERATION TODAY

The United States Soccer Federation officially represents America in the world game.

28

The United States Soccer Federation was founded in 1913 and in the same year was recognized by the Federation International de Football (FIFA) as its United States affiliate. FIFA is a world organization of more than 140 nations.

In membership with the United States Soccer Federation are 38 State Associations, the American Soccer League, the North American Soccer League, the National Soccer Coaches Association. the Intercollegiate Soccer Football Association and the United States Olympic team.

Amateur and semi-professional clubs are affiliated through their leagues with the State Association. Professional players are registered through the United States Soccer Federation and amateur players are registered through their local State Association. College and other coaches are associated with the United States Soccer Federation through the National Soccer Coaches Association. Although colleges and universities are affiliated with the national federation through the Intercollegiate Soccer Association it is only a loose liaison, as the Intercollegiate body retains autonomous control over its members, who are not subject to U.S.S.F. dictates.

The United States Soccer Federation through its FIFA membership is delegated by the American Olympic Committee with the selection and training of national teams for the Pan-American and Olympic competitions. It also provides the United States National Teams for the World Cup Competition and the International Youth Tournament.

Other functions of the United States Soccer Federation cover:

1. Supervision of international games in the United States.
2. Sponsorship of Coaching and Refereeing Schools and Clinics.
3. Conduct of the National Open Cup and National Amateur Cup Competitions.
4. Production of coaching and refereeing manuals, films, charts and rule books.

The annual meeting of the United States Soccer Federation is held each summer at a location selected by the National Commission. The headquarters of the Federation are in New York City.

The United States Soccer Federation has survived the years through the able leadership, at the top, of several outstanding individuals. Dr. G. Randolph Manning, the first president, and Thomas Cahill, the first Executive Secretary, were men of outstanding character. Cahill served from 1913 to 1930, and was succeeded by James Armstrong until 1943. Joseph Barriskill, the "Grand Old Man" of American soccer, served as Executive Secretary from 1943 to 1971.

James McGuire, six times president of the Federation, and Harry Kraus, who seven times was elected as a Vice President and who was responsible for the revival of youth soccer after World War II, also combined their efforts to bring soccer to more Americans.

Currently, Kurt Lamm, Executive Secretary, and Gene Edwards, President, with vast organizational abilities, are guiding the USSF into the modern era of the game. Phil Woosnam, as Commissioner of the North American Soccer League, is a USSF Vice President who lends reason and experience to the task of bringing different soccer interests together.

In the future, the development of the Federation and its impact on soccer in America will depend not only on these qualified men, but on their ability to find equally motivated and selfless people to carry out its many responsibilities.

29
THE UNITED STATES
SOCCER HALL OF FAME

Rugged field conditions, hardy souls, on both sides of the touchline, with industrial America in the background . . . all hallmarks of the game and those who held it together for so long.

29

The United States Soccer Federation Hall of Fame is an offshoot of the effort of the Philadelphia Old-Timers Association to identify people who had contributed as players and officials to the progress of soccer in the United States.

From 1950 until 1953 the National Soccer Hall of Fame was sponsored by the Philadelphia group, awaking a segment of the American sports public to the rich heritage of soccer in this country. Recognizing the need of a showplace with which to promote the virtues of soccer, the United States Soccer Federation at its 37th Annual Convention in 1953 at Atlantic City, New Jersey, accepted the management of the project. A Hall of Fame Committee to conduct the selection of members to be honored became a permanent part of the soccer establishment.

SOCCER HALL OF FAME MEMBERS THROUGH 1978

Alonso, Julius A. (N.Y.) 1972
Barriskill, Joseph J. (N.Y.) 1953
Andersen, William (N.Y.) 1956
Armstrong, James (N.Y.) 1952
Beardsworth, Fred (Mass.) 1965
Bernabei, Raymond (Pa.) 1978
Bahr, Walter (Pa.) 1976
Booth, Joseph (Conn.) 1952
Borghi, Frank (Mo.) 1976
Boxer, Mathew (Ca.) 1961
Brittan, Harold (Pa.) 1951
Brock, John (Mass.) 1950
Brown, Andrew M. (Ohio) 1950
Brown, David (N.J.) 1951
Cahill, Thomas W. (N.J.) 1950

Carrafi, Ralph (Ohio) 1959
Chesnew, Stanley (N.Y.) 1966
Collins, George M. (Mass.) 1951
Commander, Colin (Ohio) 1967
Colombo, Charles (Mo.) 1976
Craddock, Robert (Pa.) 1959
Craggs, Edward (Wash.) 1969
Cummings, Wilfred R. (Ill.) 1953
Donaghy, Edward J. (N.Y.) 1951
Donelli, Aldo T. (Pa.) 1954
Douglas, James E. (N.J.) 1954
Dresmich, John W. (Pa.) 1968
Dugan, Thomas (N.J.) 1955
Epperleim, Rudy (N.J.) 1951
Fairfield, Harry (Pa.) 1951

Ferguson, John (Pa.) 1950
Fernley, John A. (Mass.) 1951
Ferro, Charles (N.Y.) 1958
Fishwick, George E. (Ill.) 1974
Flamhaft, Jack (N.Y.) 1964
Fleming, Harry G. (Pa.) 1967
Foulds, Powys A. L. (Mass.) . . . 1953
Foulds, Sam T. N. (Mass.) 1969
Fowler, Daniel W. (N.Y.) 1970
Fryer, William J. (N.J.) 1951
Gaetjens, Joseph (N.Y.) 1976
Garcia, Peter (Mo.) 1964
Giesler, Walter (Mo.) 1962
Glover, Charles E. (N.Y.) 1965
Gonsalves, William (Mass.) 1950
Gould, David L. (Pa.) 1953
Govier, Sheldon (Ill.) 1950
Gryzik, Joseph (Ill.) 1973
Healy, George (Mich.) 1951
Hemmings, William (Ill.) 1961
Hudson, Maurice (Ca.) 1966
Hynes, John (N.J.) 1977
Inglehart, Alfredda (Md.) 1951
Jaap, John (Pa.) 1953
Jeffrey, William (Pa.) 1951
Johnson, Jack (Ill.) 1952
Kempton, George (Wash.) 1950
Keough, Harry (Mo.) 1976
Klein, Paul (N.J.) 1953
Koszma, Oscar (Ca.) 1964
Kraus, Harry A. (N.Y.) 1963
Kuntner, Rudy (N.Y.) 1963
Lang, Millard (Md.) 1950
Lewis, H. Edgar (Pa.) 1950
MacEwan, John J. (Mich.) 1953
McGuire, John (N.Y.) 1951
McGuire, James P. (N.Y.) 1951
McLaughlin, Bernard (Pa.) 1977
McIlveney, Edward (Pa.) 1976
Magnozzi, Enzo (N.Y.) 1978
Maca, Joseph (N.Y.) 1976
McSkimming, Den (Mo.) 1951

Maher, Jack (Ill.) 1970
Manning, Rudolf R. (N.Y.) 1950
Marre, John (Mo.) 1953
Mieth, Werner (N.J.) 1974
Millar, Robert (N.Y.) 1950
Mills, James (Pa.) 1954
Morrison, Robert (Pa.) 1951
Morrissette, William (Mass.) 1967
Netto, Fred (Ill.) 1958
Niotis, Dimitrios J. (Ill.) 1963
Olaff, Gene (N.J.) 1971
Oliver, Arnold (Mass.) 1968
Palmer, William (Pa.) 1952
Pariani, Cino (Mo.) 1976
Patenaude, Bertrand A. (Mass.) . . 1971
Peel, Peter J. (Ill.) 1951
Peters, Wally (N.J.) 1967
Pomeroy, Edgar (Ca.) 1955
Ramsden, Arnold (Texas) 1957
Ratican, Harry (Mo.) 1950
Reese, Vernon R. (Md.) 1957
Renzulli, Peter (N.Y.) 1951
Ryan, John (Pa.) 1958
Sager, Thomas (Pa.) 1968
Schields, F. (Zibikowski) (N.J.) . . 1968
Schillinger, Emil (Pa.) 1960
Schroeder, Elmer (Pa.) 1951
Scwarcz, Erno (N.Y.) 1951
Smith, Alfred (Pa.) 1951
Spalding, Richard (Pa.) 1951
Stark, Archie (N.J.) 1950
Steur, August (N.Y.) 1969
Stewart, Douglas (Pa.) 1950
Swords, Thomas (Mass.) 1951
Souza, Edward (Mass.) 1976
Souza, John (Mass.) 1976
Tintle, George (N.J.) 1952
Triner, Joseph (Ill.) 1951
Weir, Alex. (N.Y.) 1975
Weston, Victor (Wash.) 1956
Wallace, Frank (Mo.) 1976
Wilson, Peter (N.J.) 1950

Woods, John W. (Ill.) 1952
Young, John (Ca.) 1958
Zampini, Daniel (Pa.) 1963
Zerhusen (Ca.) 1978

MERITORIOUS AWARD

Abronzino, Umberto (Ca.) 1971
Ardizzone, John (Ca.) 1971
Briggs, Lawrence E. (Mass.) 1978
Cordery, Ted (Ca.) 1975
Delach, Joseph (Pa.) 1973
Duff, Duncan (Ca.) 1972
Di Orio, Nick (Pa.) 1974
Dunn, James (Mo.) 1974
Moore, James F. (Mo.) 1971
Miller, Milton (N.Y.) 1971
McGrath, Frank (Mass.) 1978
Piscopo, Giorgio (N.Y.) 1978
Rottenberg, Jack J. (N.J.) 1971
Steelink, Nicolas (Ca.) 1971
Stone, Robert T. (Co.) 1971
Walder, James A. (Pa.) 1971
Washauer, Adolph (Ca.) 1977
McClay, Allan (Mass.) 1971
Merovich, Peter (Pa.) 1971

HONORABLE MENTION

Alexander, William (Ill.) 1952
Barriskill, Joseph (N.Y.) 1952
Blakey, Albert (N.J.) 1953

Cooper, Al (N.J.) 1951
Costa, Vincent (Mass.) 1953
Cummings, Wilfred (Ill.) 1951
Donelli, Aldo (Pa.) 1952
Duffy, Edward (N.J.) 1952
Ferro, Charles (N.Y.) 1953
Foulds, Powys A. L. (Mass.) 1952
Foulds, Sam T. N. (Mass.) 1951
Giesler, Walter J. (Mo.) 1951
Gundersen, Austin S. (Wash.) . . . 1952
Govier, B. (Ill.) 1951
Guyda, Andrew 1952
Klein, Paul (N.J.) 1952
Kirkpatrick, W. (Pa.) 1951
Kraus, Harry (N.Y.) 1951
Kraus, Harry (N.Y.) 1952
Marre, John (Mo.) 1952
McKinley, James (N.Y.) 1952
Murray, Thomas (Pa.) 1951
McEwan, John J. (Mich.) 1951
O'Brien, Shamus (N.J.) 1952
O'Riordan, John (Mass.) 1952
Rever, Andrew (N.Y.) 1952
Ritchie, George (Mass.) 1951
Silovsky, Joseph (Ill.) 1952
Schuerholz, Gilbert (Md.) 1953
Scwarcz, Erno (N.Y.) 1951
Stewart, Harry (Md.) 1951
Stewart, George S. (Md.) 1952
Sweeney, P. (N.J.) 1951
Woods, John W. (Md.) 1951

The 1950 World Cup team, which shocked the world, and themselves, by defeating England at Belo Horizonte, 1-0.

APPENDIX

Walpole Street Grounds, Boston, 1926. Scott of the New York Giants heads against Barney Battles of Boston, during the "Golden Age of Soccer," when the best soccer in the world was played.

Appendix

NATIONAL YOUTH CUP WINNERS

1935 – Reliable Juniors of New Bedford, MA
1936 – Hatikvoh Juniors of Brooklyn, NY
1937 – Hatikvoh Juniors of Brooklyn, NY
1938 – Lighthouse Boys' Club of Phila., PA
1939 – Avella Juniors of Avella, PA
1940 – Avella Juniors of Avella, PA
1941 – Mercerville Juniors of Trenton, NJ
1942-1943-1944 – No competition as travel restricted because of war effort.
1945 – Hornets of Chicago, IL and Pompei Juniors of Baltimore, MD, declared co-champions.
1946 – Schumacher Juniors of St. Louis, MO
1947 – Heidelberg Juniors of Heidelberg, PA
1948 – Lighthouse Boys' Club of Phila., PA
1949 – Lighthouse Boys' Club of Phila., PA
1950 – Harrison Juniors of Harrison, NJ
1951 – Seco Juniors os St. Louis, MO
1952 – Kollsman S.C. of Brooklyn, NY
1953 – Newark Boys Club of Newark, NJ (East)
1954 – Hansa S.C. of Chicago, IL
1955 – Gottschee S.C. of Brooklyn, NY (East)
1955 – Schwaben of Chicago, IL (West)

1956 – St. Singelbert of St. Louis, MO
1957 – Lightbouse Boys' Club of Phila., PA
1958 – St. Paul of St. Louis, MO
1959 – Ukrainian of New York, NY
1960 – St. Paul of St. Louis, MO
1961 – Hakoah of San Francisco, CA
1962 – Schumacher of St. Louis, MO
1963 – Kutis of St. Louis, MO
1964 – Kutis of St. Louis, MO
1965 – I. M. Heart of Mary of St. Louis, MO
1966 – St. William of St. Louis, MO
1967 – Lighthouse Boys' Club of Phila., PA
1968 – St. Philip Di Neri of St. Louis, MO
1969 – St. Philip Di Neri of St. Louis, MO
1970 – St. Barts of St. Louis, MO
1971 – Seco of St. Louis, MO
1972 – Seco of St. Louis, MO
1973 – St. Elizabeth S.C. of Baltimore, MD
1974 – Florissant Celtics of St. Louis, MO
1975 – Imo's Pizza of St. Louis, MO
1976 – Annandae Cavaliers, VA
1977 – Santa Clara Bronc
1978 – Imo's Pizza of St. Louis, MO

NATIONAL AMATEUR CHALLENGE CUP WINNERS

*1923 – No winner – Unfinished – Weather conditions
1924 – Fleisher Yarn F.C. of Phila., PA
1925 – Toledo F.C. of Toledo, OH
1926 – Defenders F.C. of Cleveland, OH
1927 – Heidelberg S.C. of Heidelberg, PA
1928 – Swedish American F.C. of Detroit, MI and Powers Hudson Essex S.C. of Newark, NJ declared co-champions.
1929 – Heidelberg S.C. of Heidelberg, PA
1930 – Raffies F.C. of St. Louis, MO
1931 – Goodyear S.C. of Cleveland, OH

1932 – Shamrock S.C. of Cleveland, OH
1933 – German American S.C. of Phila., PA
1934 – German American S.C. of Phila., PA
1935 – W. W. Riehl S.C. of Pittsburgh, PA
1936 – Brooklyn German S.C. of Brooklyn, NY
1937 – Trenton Highlander S.C. of Trenton, NJ
1938 – Ponta Delgada S.C. of Fall River, MA
1939 – St. Michael's S.C. of Fall River, MA
1940 – Morgan Strasser S.C. of Morgan, PA
1941 – Fall River S.C. of Fall River, MA
1942 – Fall River S.C. of Fall River, MA
1943 – Morgan Strasser S.C. of Morgan, PA
1944 – Eintracht Sport Club of New York, NY

NATIONAL AMATEUR CHALLENGE CUP WINNERS (Cont.)

1945 – Eintracht Sport Club of New York, NY
1946 – Ponta Delgada S.C. of Fall River, MA
**1947 – Ponta Delgada S.C. of Fall River, MA
1948 – Ponta Delgada S.C. of Fall River, MA
1949 – Elizabeth Sport Club of Elizabeth, NJ
1950 – Ponta Delgada S.C. of Fall River, MA
**1951 – German Hungarian S.C. of N.Y., NY
1952 – Raiders S.C. of Fall River, MA
1953 – Ponta Delgada S.C. of Fall River, MA
1954 – Beadling of Beadling, PA
1955 – Heidelberg S.C. of Heidelberg, PA
1956 – Kutis S.C. of St. Louis, MO
**1957 – Kutis S.C. of St. Louis, MO
1958 – Kutis S.C. of St. Louis, MO
1959 – Kutis S.C. of St. Louis, MO
1960 – Kutis S.C. of St. Louis, MO
1961 – Kutis S.C. of St. Louis, MO

1962 – Carpathia Kickers of Detroit, MI
1963 – Italian American of Rochester, NY
1964 – Schwaben S.C. of Chicago, IL
1965 – German-Hungarian S.C. of N.Y., NY
1966 – Chicago Kickers S.C. of Chicago, IL
1967 – Hartford Italians S.C. of Hartford, CT
1968 – Chicago Kickers S.C. of Chicago, IL
1969 – British Lions S.C. of Washington, D.C.
1970 – Chicago Kickers S.C. of Chicago, IL
1971 – Kutis S.C. of St. Louis, MO
1972 – Busch S.C. of St. Louis, MO
1973 – Philadelphia Inter S.C. of Phila., PA
1974 – Philadelphia Inter S.C. of Phila., PA
1975 – Chicago Kickers S.C. of Chicago, IL
1976 – Milwaukee Barvarians
1977 – Denver Kickers
1978 – Denver Kickers

**Won both NACC and NCC

NATIONAL CHALLENGE CUP WINNERS

1914 – Brooklyn Field Club of Brooklyn, NY
1915 – Bethlehem Steel F.C. of Bethlehem, PA
1916 – Bethlehem Steel F.C. of Bethlehem, PA
1917 – Fall River Rovers of Fall River, MA
1918 – Bethlehem Steel F.C. of Bethlehem, PA
1919 – Bethlehem Steel F.C. of Bethlehem, PA
1920 – Ben Miller F.C. of St. Louis, MO
1921 – Robbins Dry Dock F.C. of Brooklyn, NY
1922 – Scullin Steel F.C. of St. Louis, MO
1923 – Paterson F.C. of Paterson, NJ
1924 – Fall River F.C. of Fall River, MA
1925 – Shawsheen F.C. of Tiverton, RI
1926 – Bethlehem Steel F.C. of Bethlehem, PA
1927 – Fall River F.C. of Fall River, MA
1928 – New York National S.C. of N.Y., NY
1929 – Hakoah All Star S.C. of New York, NY
1930 – Fall River F.C. of Fall River, MA
1931 – Fall River F.C. of Fall River, MA
1932 – New Bedford F.C. of New Bedford, MA
1933 – Stix, Baer & Fuller F.C. of St. Louis, MO
1934 – Stix, Baer & Fuller F.C. of St. Louis, MO
1935 – Central Breweries F.C. of Chicago, IL
1936 – Philadelphia American S.C. of Phila., PA
1937 – New York American F.C. of N.Y., NY
1938 – Sparta A. & B. A. of Chicago, IL
1939 – St. Mary's Celtic S.C. of Brooklyn, NY
*1940 – No winner
1941 – Pawtucket F.C. of Pawtucket, RI
1942 – Gallatin S.C. of Gallatin, PA
1943 – Brooklyn Hispano F.C. of Brooklyn, NY
1944 – Brooklyn Hispano F.C. of Brooklyn, NY
1945 – Brookhattan F.C. of New York, NY
1946 – Chicago Viking F.C. of Chicago, IL

**1947 – Ponta Delgada S.C. of Fall River, MA
1948 – Simpkins-Ford S.C. of St. Louis, MO
1949 – Morgan S.C. of Morgan, PA
1950 – Simpkins-Ford S.C. of St. Louis, MO
**1951 – German Hungarian S.C. of N.Y., NY
1952 – Harmarville S.C. of Harmerville, PA
1953 – Falcons S.C. of Chicago, IL
1954 – New York Americans of New York, NY
1955 – Eintracht of New York, NY
1956 – Harmarville S.C. of Harmarville, PA
**1957 – Kutis S.C. of St. Louis, MO
1958 – Los Angeles Kickers of Los Angeles, CA
1959 – McIlwaine Canvasbaks of
             Los Angeles, CA
1960 – National Ukrainian of Phila., PA
1961 – National Ukrainian of Phila., PA
1962 – New York Hungaria of New York, NY
1963 – National Ukrainian of Phila., PA
1964 – Los Angeles Kickers of Los Angeles, CA
1965 – New York Ukrainian of New York, NY
1966 – National Ukrainian of Phila., PA
1967 – Greek Americans of New York, NY
1968 – Greek Americans of New York, NY
1969 – Greek Americans of New York, NY
1970 – Elizabeth S.C. of Elizabeth, NJ
1971 – Hota S.C. of New York, NY
1972 – Elizabeth S.C. of Elizabeth, NJ
1973 – Maccabee S.C. of Los Angeles, CA
1974 – Greek Americans of New York, NY
1975 – Maccabee S.C. of Los Angeles, CA
1976 – San Francisco A.C.
1977 – Maccabee S.C. of Los Angeles, CA
1978 – Maccabee S.C. of Los Angeles, CA

**Won both NACC and NCC

AMERICAN CUP COMPETITION

1884-85 — O.N.T. Newark	1905-06 — West Hudsons, N.J.
86 — O.N.T. Newark	07 — East Newark Clarke A.A.
87 — O.N.T. Newark	08 — West Hudsons, N.J.
88 — Fall River Rovers	09 — Paterson True Blues
89 — Fall River Rovers	10 — Tacony F.C., Pa.
90 — Pawtucket Olympics	11 — Howard & Bullough, Pawtucket
91 — Fall River East Ends	12 — West Hudson, N.J.
92 — Fall River East Ends	13 — Paterson True Blues
93 — Pawtucket Olympics	14 — Bethlehem Steel
94 — Pawtucket Olympics	15 — Scots-Americans, N.J.
95 — Newark Caledonians	16 — Bethlehem Steel
96 — Paterson True Blues	17 — Bethlehem Steel
97 — Philadelphia Manz	18 — Bethlehem Steel
98 — Arlington F.C., N.J.	19 — No Competition
99 through 1904 — NO COMPETITION	20 — Robins Dry Dock
	21 — Robins Dry Dock
	22 — Todd Shipyard

PAST COLLEGE CHAMPIONS

NCAA DIVISION I

1959 — St. Louis
1960 — St. Louis
1961 — West Chester
1962 — St. Louis
1963 — St. Louis
1964 — Navy
1965 — St. Louis
1966 — San Francisco
1967 — Michigan State 0, St. Louis 0
    (Co-champions)
1968 — Maryland 2, Michigan State 2
    (Co-champions)
1969 — St. Louis
1970 — St. Louis
1971 — Howard 3, St. Louis 2
    (Howard vacated title for using
    ineligible player)
1972 — St. Louis
1973 — St. Louis
1974 — Howard 1, St. Louis 1
    (Co-champions)
1975 — San Francisco
1976 — San Francisco
1977 — Hartwick
1978 — San Francisco

NCAA DIVISION II

1972 — Southern Illinois
1973 — Missouri-St. Louis
1974 — Adelphi
1975 — Baltimore
1976 — Loyola (Baltimore)
1977 — Alabama A&M
1978 — Seattle Pacific

NCAA DIVISION III

1974 — SUNY-Brockport
1975 — Babson
1976 — Brandeis
1977 — Lock Haven
1978 — Lock Haven

NAIA

1959 — Pratt Institute
1960 — Elizabethtown
    Newark Engineering
    (Co-champions)
1961 — Howard
1962 — East Stroudsburg
1963 — Earlham, Castleton State
    (Co-champions)
1964 — Trenton State
1965 — Trenton State
1966 — Quincy
1967 — Quincy
1968 — Davis & Elkins
1969 — Eastern Illinois
1970 — Davis & Elkins
1971 — Quincy
1972 — Westmont
1973 — Quincy
1974 — Quincy
1955 — Quincy
1976 — Simon Fraser
1977 — Quincy
1978 — Quincy

NATIONAL INTERCOLLEGIATE SOCCER CHAMPIONS IN THE UNITED STATES — 1905 TO 1961

DETERMINED BY THE INTERCOLLEGIATE ASSOCIATION FOOTBALL LEAGUE

1904-05*	Haverford	1915	Haverford
1905-06	Haverford	1916	Pennsylvania
1906-07	Haverford	1917	Haverford
1907-08	Haverford-Yale	1918	No Competition
1908-09	Columbia	1919	Pennsylvania
1909-10	Columbia	1920	Pennsylvania
1910-11	Haverford	1921	Princeton
1911-12	Yale	1922	Princeton
1912-13	Harvard	1923	Pennsylvania
1913-14	Harvard	1924	Pennsylvania
1914**	Pennsylvania	1925	Princeton

DETERMINED BY THE INTERCOLLEGIATE SOCCER FOOTBALL ASSOCIATION

1926	Haverford	1934	Cornell
	Penn State	1935	Yale
	Princeton	1936	Penn State+
1927	Princeton		Princeton
1928	Yale***		Syracuse
1929	Penn State		West Chester
1930	Harvard	1937	Penn State
	Pennsylvania		Princeton
	Yale		Springfield
1931	Pennsylvania	1938	Penn State
1932	Pennsylvania	1939	Penn State
	Navy		Princeton
1933	Pennsylvania	1940	Penn State
	Penn State		Princeton

DETERMINED BY THE NATIONAL SOCCER COACHES ASSOCIATION

1941	Springfield++	1944	Navy
	Rider	1945	Yale
	Temple		Haverford
	Amherst		Army
1942	Amherst		Navy
	Princeton	1946	Springfield
	Rennselaer Poly	1947	Springfield
	Springfield	1948	Connecticut
1943	Rennselaer Poly		
	Navy		

DETERMINED BY THE INTERCOLLEGIATE SOCCER FOOTBALL ASSOCIATION

1949	Penn State	1955	Penn State
	San Francisco		Brockport State
1950	West Charter	1956	Trinity
1951	Temple	1957	Springfield
1952	Franklin & Marshall		CCNY
1953	Temple	1958	Drexel
1954	Penn State		

DETERMINED BY THE NATIONAL COLLEGIATE CHAMPIONSHIP

1959	St. Louis	1961	West Chester
1960	St. Louis		

---

*Not Listed in MCAA Guides after 1937.

**Changed to Fall season.

***Swarthmore, undefeated, untied, claimed co-champions in Middle-Atlantic area.

+No award through 1940; listed as outstanding teams.

++No award, undefeated, untied teams listed until 1944.

NORTH AMERICAN SOCCER LEAGUE CHAMPIONS

1967	Los Angeles	1971	Dallas Tornado
	(United Soccer Association)	1972	New York Cosmos
	Oakland	1973	Philadelphia Atoms
	(National Professional Soccer	1974	Los Angeles Aztecs
	Association)	1975	Tampa Bay Rowdies
1968	Atlanta Chiefs	1976	Toronto Metros
1969	Kansas City Chiefs	1977	New York Cosmos
1970	Rochester Lancers	1978	New York Cosmos

AMERICAN SOCCER LEAGUE CHAMPIONS

1934	Kearny Irish	1957	New York Hakoah
1935	Philadelphia Germans	1958	New York Hakoah
1936	New York Americans	1959	New York Hakoah
1937	Kearny Scots	1960	Colombo
1938	Kearny Scots	1961	Ukranian Nationals
1939	Kearny Scots	1962	Ukranian Nationals
1940	Kearny Scots	1963	Ukranian Nationals
1941	Kearny Scots	1964	Ukranian Nationals
1942	Philadelphia Americans	1965	Hartford S.C.
1943	Brooklyn Hispanos	1966	Roma S.C.
1944	Philadelphia Americans	1967	Baltimore St. Gerard's
1945	New York Brookhattan	1968	Ukranian Nationals
1946	Baltimore Americans	1968	Washington Darts
1947	Philadelphia Americans	1969	Washington Darts
1948	Philadelphia Americans	1970	Philadelphia Ukranians
1949	Philadelphia Nationals	1971	New York Greeks
1950	Philadelphia Nationals	1972	Cincinnati Comets
1951	Philadelphia Nationals	1973	New York Apollo
1952	Philadelphia Americans	1974	Rhode Island Oceaneers
1953	Philadelphia Nationals	1975	Boston Astros-New York Apollos
1954	New York Americans	1976	Los Angeles Skyhawks
1955	Uhrik Truckers	1977	New Jersey Americans
1956	Uhrik Truckers	1978	New York Apollos

UNITED STATES NATIONAL TEAM MEMBERS (Senior)

Since 1913, teams of players representing the National Team of the United States have played against National Teams from other countries. In these 85 games, four hundred and forty two (442) players have participated in these contests. In the interests of soccer history, and in recognition of their achievements, these players are listed here:

Bayard Abaunza	WC-68	George Brown	WC-57, PA-59
Manuel Abaunza	WC-68	James Brown	WC-30
Robert Aitken	O-28	Ernie Buck	T-55
Dietrich Albright	WC-68	Walt Burgin	T-16
Antone Almeida	T-49	Robert Burkhardt	O-52, WC-57
Charles Altemose	O-36	Gordon Burness	T-26
Thomas Amrheim	WC-34	Carlos Bustamente	T-61
R. Andrews	T-25	John Calcaterra	PA-63
Robert Annis	O-48, WC-50	Fred Cameron	WC-66, T-59
George Athenois	T-53	John Carden	T-37
Andy Auld	WC-30, T-26	Joe Carenza	O-72
Adolf Bachmeier	WC-68, WC-69, O-64,	James Carlton	T-37
	PA-63, T-61, T-59	William Carnihan	T-25, T-26
Casey Bahr	O-72	William Carson	T-59
Chris Bahr	O-72, T-75	Con Casey	WC-54, T-54
Walter Bahr	O-48, WC-50, WC-57,	Ifrain Chacurian	T-43, WC-54, T-54
	T-49, T-52, T-53,	Robert Chambers	T-37
	T-55, WC-54, T-54	George Chapla	O-75
Gerry Baker	WC-68	A. Chimielewski	T-37
Boris Bandov	WC-76, T-78, T-79,	J. Chimielewski	O-36
	T-77	Walter Chyzowych	WC-66
Francis Bartkus	O-36	Ben Cinowitz	T-59
Barry Barto	T-73, T-74	Joseph Clark	T-79
Barney Battles	T-25, T-26	Neil Clark	T-16
William Baxter	T-54	Ed Clear	WC-68
Ray Beckman	O-48	Ronald Coder	O-56, PA-59
Ed Begley	O-36	Paul Coffer	T-79
Dan Bell	PA-63	Neil Cohen	O-75
Tony Bellinger	T-77, T-79	Charles Columbo	O-48, O-52, WC-50,
William Bello	T-49		T-49, T-52
James Benedek	WC-68, O-68, PA-67	M. Connelly	T-53
William Bertani	O-48	Con Cosep	T-54
J. Best	T-79, T-73	Wm. Conterio	O-59, O-52
Helmut Bicek	WC-66, WC-62	Elwood Cook	O-52, O-59, WC-57,
Albert Blakely	T-16		PA-59
John Bocwinski	O-72	Jeff Coombes	WC-50
Anthony Bonezzi	T-61	Al Cooper	O-28, T-37
Mich Bookie	WC-30	Harry Cooper	T-16
Frank Borghi	WC-50, T-49, T-52,	D. Consuckian	T-73, T-74
	WC-54	Dan Counce	WC-76, T-74
Ivan Borodiak	T-64	Robert Craddock	WC-50, T-52, T-54
Jesse Braga	T-47	James Crockett	O-36
Otto Brand	O-68, PA-67	John Cronin	O-48
Ben Brewster	T-73	John Currie	T-37
David Bric	T-79	Ed Czerkiewicz	WC-34
Aage Brix	O-24	Andy Cziata	WC-66
David Brown	T-25, T-26	Sam Dalrymple	O-24

Stephen Darr	PA-63	Mike Flater	WC-76, O-72, T-75,
C. Davis	T-25		T-77
Ricky Davis	T-79, T-77	Thomas Florie	WC-30, WC-34, T-25
Irvine Davis	O-24	James Ford	T-16
John Deal	O-28	Paterson Ford	WC-57
Otto Decker	WC-57	Leroy Franks	WC-57
Rolf Decker	T-53, T-54, T-55	Steven Frank	T-73
Leo Defort	O-64	Wm. Freitag	T-61, WC-62
James Delgado	T-47	Werner Fricker	O-64, O-68, PA-67
Gary Delong	W-66, WC-68, O-64,	Santiago Formoso	WC-76, O-75
	O-68, PA-67	C. Fowles	T-79, T-77
William Demko	O-24	Joseph Gaetjens	WC-50
Robert Denton	O-36	James Gallagher	O-28, WC-30, WC-34
Buzz Demling	O-72, T-74	Bob Ganzler	WC-68, O-64, O-68,
Dave D'Errico	T-73, T-74, T-75,		PA-63, PA-67
	WC-76, T-77	Justo Garcia	T-64
Angelo DiBernardo	T-79	Gino Gardassanich	WC-50
Walter Dick	WC-34	Steve Gay	O-72
Matt Diederichsen	T-16	Gene Geimer	T-73
Nick DiOrio	WC-50, T-49	Carl Gentile	WC-68, O-64
Tino Domingues	T-75	James Gentile	WC-30
Aldo Donelli	WC-34	Victor Gerley	WC-66
Tony Donlic	T-77	Rudy Getzinger	WC-73, O-68, PA-67,
George Dorian	O-56		T-73
James Douglas	WC-30, O-24, T-25	M. Goldie	T-25
Don Droege	T-77	Robert Gormley	T-54
John Dubienny	T-37	Billy Gonsalves	WC-30, WC-34
John Duffy	O-28	Gene Grabowski	WC-57, O-59, PA-59
John Dunn	O-52	Rolf Granger	WC-57, O-59, PA-59
Don Ebert	T-79	Heinz Greet	O-64
Charles Ellis	T-16	Rolf Grienger	WC-57, O-59
Alex Ely	WC-66, O-59, PA-59,	Frank Grienert	O-36, T-37
	T-64, WC-62	Steve Grivnow	O-48, WC-54
Ed Emberger	WC-54	Fred Grgurev	WC-76, T-73
Sveld Engedahl	WC-57, O-56	Joseph Gryzik	PA-63
Bill Eppy	WC-57, O-68, PA-63	Alex Guild	O-59, PA-59
Gary Etherington	T-77, T-78, T-79	Andrew Guyda	O-36
Bert Evans	T-59	Richard Hall	T-73
Derek Evans	T-79	Ray Hamilton	T-37
Henry Farrell	O-24	Alan Hamlyn	T-75
Doug Farquar	T-59	Joseph Hamm	O-72
Sandy Fehr	WC-68	Al Harker	WC-34
J. Ferguson	T-16, T-25	Ed Hart	O-24
Thompson Ferguson	T-37	Larry Hausmann	WC-68, O-64, PA-63
Andy Ferko	T-37	John Heminsley	T-16
Joseph Ferriera	O-48, T-47	William Herd	T-25
Jack Ferris	T-55	Manny Hernandez	O-72, T-74
Dieter Ficken	O-68, PA-67	Julius Hjulian	WC-34
William Fiedler	WC-34, O-36	Ray Hornberger	O-24
William Findlay	O-24, O-28	Charles Horvath	T-64
Joseph Fink	T-73, T-75	Bruce Hudson	O-75
Ken Finn	T-61, WC-62	Larry Hulcer	T-79
Carl Fister	WC-62	Anatole Hulewsky	O-75
Stephen Flamhaft	PA-63	John Hynes	T-49

Michael Ivanow	O-68, O-72, T-73, T-74, T-75	Joe Martinelli	WC-34, T-37
		John Mason	WC-76
Arthur Jethon	PA-63	W. Mata	T-73
Carl Johnson	O-24	A. Mate	T-64
F. B. Jones	O-24	Peter Matevich	T-49
William Joseph	T-37	Bob Matteson	T-74
John Kane	O-28	Alan Mayer	T-77
Robert Kehoe	WC-66	Arnie Mausser	WC-76, T-78, T-79, T-75
Andy Keir	O-52		
James Kelly	T-25	Sam McAlee	T-37
Harry Keough	WC-50, WC-57, O-52, O-56, T-53, T-54, T-55, WC-54	Jim McAlister	T-79, T-77
		Pat McBride	WC-69, WC-72, O-64
		Chas. McCulley	T-73, T-75
Ty Keough	T-79	John McEwan	T-37
F. Kerr	T-26	T. McFarlane	T-25
Jack Kineally	O-68, PA-67	Bart McGhee	WC-30
Helmut Kofler	WC-68	John McGuire	T-25
F. Kovacs	T-73	Ebby McHugh	O-52
Myron Krash	O-68, PA-63, PA-67	Ed McIlvenney	WC-50
Nick Krat	WC-68	Mark McKain	T-74
Cornell Kreiger	WC-66	Bernard McLaughlin	O-48, WC-57, T-49, T-52, T-54, T-55, T-53
Joseph Krische	T-61, WC-62		
Martin Krumm	O-52		
P. Kulisthenko	T-59	William McLean	WC-34
Rudolf Kuntner	O-28	Doug McMillan	T-73
Kurt Kuykendall	O-75	Rueben Mendoza	WC-57, O-59, O-52, T-54
Steve Larkin	T-37		
Jake Lawrence	T-37	Shep Messing	O-72
William Lehman	WC-34	Carlos Metidieri	T-73
Hans Liotart	T-75	H. Meyerdierks	T-25
Ray Littley	O-28	Joseph Michaels	T-37, T-47
Mark Liveric	T-78, T-79	Helmut Michel	T-61
Jack Lloyd	T-37	Ole Mickelson	T-79
Wm. Looby	O-56, O-59, WC-57, WC-54, T-55, T-59, T-54	Alex Milhalovic	T-77
		Bob Miller	T-25
		Peter Miller	WC-68
Tim Loguish	T-75	Ray Milne	T-53
Vin Luciana	T-47	Val Missialoski	T-37
Fred Lutkefelder	O-36	Frank Moniz	T-47
Thomas Lynch	WC-34	Lloyd Monsen	O-52, O-56, T-55
John Lyons	O-28	Ian Moore	T-53
Alan Maca	T-73, T-75	Johnny Moore	WC-72, T-74
Joseph Maca	WC-50	Geo. Moorehouse	WC-30, WC-34, T-26
John Machado	T-47	W. Morris	T-26
Joe Machado	T-47	Joe Morrone	T-79
Barry Mahy	T-73	John Mueller	O-68, PA-67
Ron Maierhofer	PA-59	Jakes Mulholland	O-24
Greg Makowski	T-79	Edward Murphy	O-56, O-59, WC-57, WC-66, WC-68, PA-59, PA-63, WC-62, T-55, T-57, T-59, T-61, T-64
Don Malinowski	WC-54, T-55, T-54		
Make Margoulis	O-72		
Al Marino	O-56, T-55		
J. Marshall	T-26		
Joseph Martin	T-47	John Murphy	T-37
Manuel Martin	O-48, T-49	J. Murphy	WC-57

Joseph Murphy	O-28
R. Murphy	WC-57
Thomas Murray	T-16
Glen Myernick	O-75, T-78, T-79, T-77
Derek Nash	T-55
George Nemchik	O-36, T-37
Werner Nilsen	WC-34
G. Nanchoff	T-78, T-79, T-77
L. Nanchoff	T-78
Henry Noga	WC-62
Tom Norris	T-37
Henry O'Carroll	O-28
John O'Connell	T-52, WC-54
Fred O'Connor	O-24
Arnold Oliver	WC-30
Len Oliver	O-68, PA-63
John Olthaus	O-36
Hugh O'Neill	T-73
Matt O'Sullivan	O-75
Vic Ottobini	O-59, PA-59, T-59
Ed Packer	O-56
Joszef Pal	WC-68
Cino Pariani	O-48, WC-50
Steve Pecher	WC-76, T-77, T-78, T-79
Val Pelizzaro	WC-57, PA-59
Fred Pereira	T-77
Gene Petramie	WC-54
Peter Pietras	WC-34, O-36
Paul Pigoni	PA-63
John Pinezich	T-55
Telmo Pires	O-75, T-75
Jim Pollihan	WC-76, T-78, T-77
Andy Racz	T-64
Alex Rae	T-37
Steve Ralbovsky	WC-76, T-77, T-78
Herman Rapp	WC-34
Joseph Rego	O-48, T-47
Michael Renshaw	T-73
Tibor Reszneki	WC-66
James Rhody	O-24
Horst Rick	T-64
Bob Rigby	O-74, T-73, T-74, T-75
Andres Rio	T-64
Richard Roberts	T-52
D. Robertson	T-25
James Robertson	T-16
Alex Roboostoff	WC-72, O-68, O-72, O-75, PA-67, T-74
Angel Rodrigues	T-37
Joseph Roe	T-37
Con Roels	WC-57
Geo. Romanenko	PA-59
Walt Romanowicz	T-47
Walter Ronge	PA-63, T-61
Bob Rooney	WC-57
Dean Rosow	O-75
Kyle Rote, Jr.	T-73, T-74
Werner Roth	T-73, T-74, T-75
Alf Rothstein	T-37
Willy Roy	WC-66, WC-68, T-73
Art Rudd	O-24
Ed Ruddy	T-37
John Rudge	O-28
Bruce Rudroff	T-79
Jacob Ruscheinski	PA-59, O-59
Ernie Rushscherer	O-68, O-67
Francis Ryan	O-28, O-36, WC-34
Andy Rymarczuk	T-79, T-78
Myro Rys	WC-76, T-78
Hugo Salcedo	O-72
Len Salvemini	O-75, T-79
William Schaller	O-52, PA-59
John Schlenker	O-68, PA-67
Walt. Schmomotolocha	WC-66
Tom Schultz	T-53
Mike Seerey	O-72
Manfred Seissler	T-73
William Sheppell	O-52, T-49, WC-54, T-54
Jorge Siega	T-73
Joseph Silvosky	T-49
Alex Skotarek	WC-76
Mich Slavin	WC-30
Phil Slone	WC-30
Bob Smith	O-76, WC-76, T-73, T-74, T-75
Clarence Smith	T-16
E. Smith	T-26
Harry Smith	O-28
Ed Smolinski	T-55
Zenon Smylyk	O-56, O-59, WC-57, O-63, PA-59, T-61, WC-62
Joe Speca	O-59, PA-59
Terry Springthorpe	WC-57, T-53
Jos. Sokoteski	T-37
Alex Sonnenblick	PA-59
Ed Souza	O-48, WC-50, T-49, T-52, T-54, WC-54
John Souza	O-48, WC-50, O-52, T-47, T-54, WC-54
C. H. Spalding	T-16
Jim Stachrowsky	PA-59
Neil Stam	O-68, O-72, PA-67
James Stamatis	T-79

Archie Stark	T-25	Ray Voltz	T-37
T. Stark	T-25	Frank Wallace	WC-56, T-49
Gary St. Clair	O-75	Doug Wark	T-75
Horst Stemke	O-68, O-72, PA-67	Bob Wason	O-64
J. Stock	T-79	Ben Watman	T-49
Fred Stoll	O-36	Robert Watson	O-68, PA-67
Andy Straden	O-24	Herman Wecke	O-56, O-59, WC-57,
John Stremlau	O-75		PA-59, T-47, T-54
Arch. Strimmel	O-48	Herb Wells	O-24
Siegfried Stritzl	WC-68, PA-63, T-73	Kevin Welsh	O-75, T-74, T-75
Larry Surrock	O-52	J. Whitehead	WC-57
Uwe Swart	T-64	Richard Wild	T-64
Rich Sweinart	O-64	Al Wilson	T-37
Thomas Swords	T-16	Raymond Wilson	PA-59
Arpad Sziepos	O-68, PA-67	W. Wilson	T-26
George Tintle	T-16	M. Winter	T-73
Gene Tober	WC-68	Siegbert Wirth	O-56
Raphael Tracey	WC-30	Dennis Wit	WC-76, O-75, T-79
John Traina	O-59, PA-59, T-57,	Adam Wolanin	WC-50, O-64, T-61
	T-61, WC-62	Alex Woods	WC-30
John Travis	T-47	Myron Worober	O-68, PA-67
Al Trost	O-72, T-74, WC-76,	Wolfgang Worti	O-64
	T-78	Nelson Yableski	T-64
Roy Turner	T-73	Lou Takopec	WC-57
Edward Valentine	T-47	Robert Yarson	T-37
Rolf Valtin	O-48	Rudy Ybarra	T-79
Perry Van Der Beck	T-79	Fred Zbilowski	O-36
Denny Vanninger	T-74	Al Zerhusen	WC-57, WC-66, O-56,
Fred Vasquez	O-64		PA-57, O-59, T-57,
Frank Vaughn	WC-30		T-61, WC-62
Julie Veee	WC-76	Wally Ziaja	WC-73, O-72, T-73
Gene Ventrigcia	O-68, PA-67	Jim Zylker	O-75, T-75
G. Villa	T-78, T-77	John Zywan	O-36

```
Key:  WC    World Cup Games
      O     Olympic Games
      PA    Pan American Games
      T     International Games vs.
            other nations in challenge
            games

Example:
      WC-50    World Cup 1950
```

Thanks to the following, who aided in photo research, and who provided material:

George Bailey, George M. Collins, Walter Dick, John Ferguson, Arthur Foulds, Dianne Foulds, John Foulds, Pal Foulds, Sam Foulds, Jr., Stephen Foulds, Richard Giebner, Gabe Lovy, Thomas Murray, Oto Maxmilian, Don Rogers, Jack Rottenberg, and James Walder.